FUM D'ESTAMPA PRESS

ENGLISH HOURS

'As choice as a 5 o'clock cup of tea.'
El País

'A book that has contributed greatly to Catalan memoir
writing, normalising it while at the same time elevating it to
its highest climbs.'
Lluís Bonada, El Temps

'Soldevila shows a great mind, an interesting life and a
fascinating story. An excellent book.'
Carles Ribera, Presència

'Read at the beginning of the 21st century, English Hours
represents not only the rediscovering of a piece of writing
once lost to culture, but also the necessity to connect this
uncertain present with a brighter past, its "European tone"
that can still provide us with many lessons for the future.'
Francesc Foguet i Boreu, Llengua & Literatura

About the Authors

Ferran Soldevila (1894-1971) was a professional Catalan historian who also enjoyed success as a poet and dramatist. Seconded from the University of Barcelona, he went in 1926 on a two-year posting as Spanish language assistant at Liverpool University. On returning to Barcelona he was actively engaged in the cultural dimension of Catalanist politics in the turbulent years leading to the Spanish Civil War and subsequently the Franco dictatorship. His standing in the Catalan literary pantheon has been enhanced in recent years, as the appearance of this translation of his English journal testifies.

Alan Yates, born in Northampton in 1944, studied Modern Languages at the University of Cambridge. From 1968 he taught in the Department of Hispanic Studies at the University of Sheffield where he was promoted in 1990 to a personal Chair in Catalan Studies. Early retirement in 1999 enabled him to cultivate his enthusiasm for literary translation (exclusively Catalan-English), for which he has been awarded various distinctions.

English Hours

FERRAN SOLDEVILA

Translation by Alan Yates

FUM D'ESTAMPA PRESS LTD.

Hores angleses
© Heirs of Ferran Soldevila
© 2011, Adesiara Editorial

This translation has been published in Great Britain
by Fum d'Estampa Press Limited 2020

001

Translation copyright © Alan Yates, 2019

The moral right of the author and translator has been asserted
Set in Minion Pro by Raimon Benach

Printed and bound by TJ International Ltd, Padstow, Cornwall
A CIP catalogue record for this book is available from the British Library

Fum d'Estampa Press is grateful to all at Adesiara Editorial for their invaluable help

ISBN: 978-1-9162939-2-2

Series cover design has been inspired by the *rajola catalana*, a traditional
terracotta tile design used throughout the region.

Fum d'Estampa Press is dedicated to promoting and celebrating
Catalan culture, literature and language.

FUM D'ESTAMPA PRESS

www.fumdestampa.com

Contents

Translator's Perspective

The rewards of being enabled to 'see ourselves as others see us' can be subtly enhanced when the tense is adjusted to '… as others saw us'. This English version of a Catalan scholar's stay in England over the two academic years 1926–28 offers a particular case in point.

Ferran Soldevila (Barcelona 1894–1971) was an intellectual whose lifetime spanned a period of momentous changes in his own society, from the earliest manifestations of Catalan cultural and eventually political 'rebirth', through the agitated context of fundamental conflict with the Spanish state culminating in the Civil War (1936–39) whose outcome was thirty years of centralist oppression under the Franco regime.

Soldevila's work as academic historian culminated in his monumental *Història de Catalunya* (1934–35). He was exiled in France after the Spanish Civil War until his return to Barcelona in 1943, when his academic activities were resumed under the aegis of a parallel University organisation, Estudis Universitaris Catalans, which had been revived in 1941 and operated clandestinely until 1950. He did not live to see the eventual 'transition to democracy' in Spain after the death of the dictator Franco in 1975.

The gestation of the original publication of Soldevila's *Hores angleses* was fundamentally conditioned by contemporary political circumstances at home after his return to Barcelona from Liverpool, where he had occupied the post of lector in Spanish at the University. Some of his entries appeared in the Catalan press during the final years of the earlier centralist dictatorship in Spain (1923–30) of General Primo de Rivera. As 'cultural resistance' became increasingly the only means of expression for Catalanist aspirations, he was encouraged to prepare a book-length compilation. The dating of his Preface (1929) corresponds to this phase.

That *Hores angleses* was not finally published until 1938 is explained by the turbulence in Spain during the period of the second Spanish Republic (1930–36) and the Civil War of 1936–39. Throughout that decade Catalonia, with its 'federalist' political programme, became the main defender and ultimately the last bastion of the Republic. Just as earlier under Primo de Rivera but now even more urgently, cultural resistance represented the last-ditch defensive response to centralism and totalitarianism. The date of publication (1938, in a collection sponsored by the beleaguered Catalan government, last bastion of the Spanish Republic) and the 'austerity' quality of the paper lend poignancy to the representative status of the original edition of *Hores angleses*.

Soldevila was an assiduous private diarist, and the entire body of his autobiographical writing was edited and incorporated in the substantial volume of memoirs entitled *Al llarg de la meva vida/Throughout My Life* (1970). That compilation contains some supplementary diary entries which are directly relevant to this edition of *Hores angleses/English Hours*, relating to the circumstances of the author's appointment at Liverpool University. Of particular interest among these jottings is mention of the roles of Joan Estelrich[1] and the eminent British Hispanist Edgar Allison Peers[2] in setting up the arrangement.

Also documented are Soldevila's initial anxiety in contemplating the imminent displacement to England, some observations on the railway journey through France and, at the very beginning of taking up his new post, the resolution to write up his English experiences:

Liverpool, 13 October 1926

In my University diary I have started to make notes. These, together with other jottings on things here and together with some memories which will not be written down, will be the basis of my Impressions of a Stay in England, which some time in the future I shall write.

In July 1929 the Catalan newspaper La Publicitat carried an article by Salvador Dalí, where the artist proclaimed:

'I can prophesy that, in documentary terms, any old album

1   Joan Estelrich (1896–1958).Conservative Catalanist intellectual and writer. He was engaged in the institutional promotion of Catalan culture and occupied official positions from which he could promote internationally the Catalan case for recognition as a 'small nation' after the 1914–1918 War. His activity on this front formed part of Catalan political opposition to the Spanish military government (1923–30) of Primo de Rivera.

2   Edgar Allison Peers (1891–1952). First Gilmour Professor of Spanish at Liverpool University from 1922 until his death. His book *Catalonia Infelix* (1937) concerns the Civil War and betokens his great interest in Catalan culture and politics, with many important contacts there.

displaying post-cards of street scenes and squares in Paris will one day have more value than all of the literary descriptions of the same places done by the very best writers. Nor will such descriptions have any spiritual value. All that will ultimately count will be exclusively the surrealist documents and texts of the present day.'

This was published only six months after Ferran Soldevila was appending the final, retrospective sections to his own book of 'literary descriptions' centred on a particular European city at a particular time. The appearance now of our version of his *English Hours* makes it possible for a new readership to assess the 'documentary' and 'spiritual' qualities of a work which seems to embody virtually everything against which the surrealist was railing. These readers will likewise be able to judge whether *English Hours* can 'count' nowadays for anything.

Soldevila the professional historian, whose brother Carles was a successful novelist, also had a literary vocation, principally for poetry, and this shows through in *Hores angleses*. The longest sections of the book are, not surprisingly, the accounts of his visits as a conventional, though very cultivated, foreign visitor to places (London, Edinburgh and the Highlands, Oxford, etc.) renowned as major attractions. But these entries are punctuated by shorter day-to-day observations on his work at the university, his everyday routines, insights into English life and manners, etc., areas of experience accessible only to someone spending a relatively long period, becoming integrated in the new milieu, and living normal life as a temporary resident in his employment at the University and residence in the staid suburbia of the Wirral.

There is a visible 'imbalance' throughout the work between the lengthiest entries, mainly touristic, and some very much more condensed, even telegraphic, ones. Many of the latter give the impression of being mere jottings intended for subsequent elaboration (as the author mentions in his preface).

On the other hand, there are others that have the appearance, or give the feel, of being deliberate 'poetic' distillations of something observed, a sensation or a particular mood. The entry for the 30 October 1926 comprises a five-stanza complete poem, but many other 'unprocessed' jottings in prose seem to point in the same direction, between the delicate evocation of Christmas Day 1926 and the verbal snapshot of a Liverpool Sunday afternoon (27 May 1928).

Underlying the minimalist 'impressionism' of so many of the short entries is a note of melancholy which sounds faintly but insistently through the cumulative effect. It turns upon the feeling of *enyorança* (akin to but more subtle than melancholy homesickness), which can be subject to delicate modulations as in the conclusion to the author's evocation of Edinburgh (16 June 1927): 'A gentle sort of sweetness dominates the feeling of being so far away from your own latitudes, a sort of sweetness which is the inversion of nostalgia or longing for home.' Only four days after first arriving in London and residing now in West Kirby, the thrill of the author's new circumstances elicits a feeling of 'happiness' at being installed in comfortable surroundings, but he will not allow himself to 'speak too soon' (7 October 1926), as though anticipating that difficulties of acclimatisation lie ahead.

Understandably, homesickness as a natural correlative of cultural displacement is expressed more frequently in the earlier period of the author's residence in England, as is delicately depicted in his explicit response (23 February 1927) to Hilaire Belloc's poem on the 'South Country'. In the same phase this feeling is projected onto or mirrored in encounters with other foreigners that come into Soldevila's personal horizon, like those met at the university: the Russian lector (23 November 1926 and 22 February 1927) and the two French lectrices (11 February 1927). His travelling by public transport, of which he did plenty, is also a natural setting for significant encounters. In the same vein as the examples just referred to is the episode of the talkative Madrilenian in the train compartment (14 January 1927), and the subtly skewed conclusion: 'A sort of gentle sweetness dominates the feeling of being so far away from your own latitudes: a sort of sweetness which is the inversion of nostalgia or home-sickness.'

This theme is engaged with in two lengthy entries focused on literary themes, in the setting of separate visits to the British Museum library, which occupy strategic prominence in the book. Each illustrates the concept of *enyorança*, yearning for something out of reach, associated with nostalgia for a time or a place. The first evokes a close friend, a distinguished poet, whose memory is associated for Soldevila with 'the countryside where I myself was made to feel I was a poet' (12 April 1927).[3] This entry is balanced by the lengthy account a year later (2 May 1928) of his discovering in a local library Hepburn Ballantine's extremely rare *A Crusade into Catalonia*

---

3   Jaume Bofill i Mates (Olot 1888–Barcelona 1933), politician and poet who used the literary pseudonym of Guerau de Liost. He was active in the phase of Catalan cultural nationalism in the first decades of the 20th century. An intimate friend of Soldevila, they shared a love for the mountain district of the Montseny, where each of them had a house, Bofill in Viladrau, and Soldevila in nearby Paulautordera.

(1894). Soldevila ends his encomium of that account of a walking tour in the eastern Pyrenees with an emotional tribute, evoking a frontispiece photogravure portrait of the author: 'Ah! Hepburn Ballantine, you of the kindly oval face, of the bushy white whiskers hiding your mouth like a thick veil, of the gentle but slightly mischievous look, if you were still alive today, I would go to your sad suburb in the dark city of Birkenhead and I would shake you warmly by the hand.' Ironically this author is nowadays better known in Catalonia than in his own country. His self-published book has virtually disappeared into total oblivion at home, while a Catalan translation was published in 1994.

Some of the 'unevenness' and variety of registers in Soldevila's journal can be attributed to the relatively long period of his stay in the United Kingdom and the purely practical demands of keeping a record of experiences and impressions over that period, with all the diverse distractions of residing (and sightseeing) abroad. The author lived through the jazz era, and syncopation as a feature of modernity (and of modernism) can certainly be taken into account. Even more than Soldevila's contemporaries, 21st-century readers are accustomed to taking in and interpreting 'broken' or multi-level literary discourse. Thus the author's explanation or apology for the character of his 'unfinished' book is less necessary for his readers of today than for those originally envisaged by him...

Saying that *Hores angleses* is a 'dated' text acquires diverse nuances in the light of what has been explained up to this point. From his disembarking in Dover, in October 1926, through to his reflections of September 1928 on the rigorous efficiency of the British tax system, today's reader perceives the reality evoked by Soldevila and the presence of his autobiographical persona as though in sequences of grainy black and white photographs or in newsreel footage from that time: dark suit and shiny black shoes, white shirt with starched collar, complemented by a long, heavy overcoat for out of doors, and probably a trilby hat. We are responding to the 'discreet charm' that many new readers of today will find for themselves in the author's literary distillation of his experiences as an 'outsider' in the England of the late 1920s.

Returning to Dalí's diatribe against travel writing quoted earlier: our translation of *Hores angleses* will have the utility, at least, of enabling an English-language readership to form an opinion on whether Soldevila's book has any 'spiritual value' and whether it 'counts' for anything...

English Hours

FERRAN SOLDEVILA

The Diary of a Catalan Historian in Liverpool, 1926-28

Soldevila's footnotes are indicated by *, as in the original.

The translator's notes are numbered.

Introductory note to the 1938 edition

This is a book which is not fully finished, or at least which appears now in a form quite different from the one originally envisaged. I lived in England – Lecturer in Spanish at the University of Liverpool – during the academic years 1926–1928, taking notes and collecting material with the intention of writing my impressions of the country and putting them together in one volume. A number of articles responding to this objective were given space in the pages of *La Publicitat* and *Mirador*.[1] I even had a part of the preface already written, and that text, as it then stood, follows this preliminary note. But my *Història de Catalunya* for Editorial Alpha was an immensely time-consuming undertaking which obliged me to abandon the other project. That was eight years ago, and now I find myself too far removed from the original to rework and complete it: some of the material I had gathered

1   *La Publicitat*: daily newspaper which in 1922 became the organ of the left-leaning Catalan nationalist party Acció Catalana which Soldevila supported. Many leading writers and thinkers of the contemporary intellectual vanguard contributed to its pages. It was closed by the Franco regime in 1939. *Mirador*: fortnightly journal of culture and ideas addressed to liberal sectors of Catalan society. Founded in 1929, it was requisitioned by the Communists early in the Spanish Civil War (1936) and ceased publication in 1938.

– newspaper cuttings, booklets, prospectuses, etc. – has lost at least part of its suggestiveness; one's memory, although reliable, is not enough to bring back to life notes that were excessively schematic; some other jottings must have been lost (thus, for example, I have found hardly any of my impressions of London). In a word, life goes on and other activities seem to beckon me.

Thus, I have confined myself to bringing together the majority of passages already written, to selecting from my diary a number of sections in note form and to filling out some details. Those elements combined form this book. My idea has been that, all in all, there could still be something of interest in it.

F. S.

Preface

April 1929

Reader:

Although these notes may often take on an autobiographical cast, nothing is further from my intentions than to supply fragments from my own autobiography. The reason why this book appears to belong generally to that class of writing is because the autobiographical form makes my job easier and facilitates presentation of impressions gathered during my stay in England. This approach re-awakens memories in step with narrative progression while steering me clear of generalisations which would be too audacious to be founded upon such a limited experience. To judge a country, and even more its people –and a people like the English– is such a delicate task that I would not dare to enter upon it except in some readily approachable aspects. I envy the talent of those who with just a glance –a few days travelling and some basic reading– are equipped to set about classifying nations and pointing out their characteristics, both the obvious and the abstruse ones. And I confess that, although I embark happily on writing up some of my memories of England (while keeping some others, naturally, for my own private recall), I also undertake the task with a certain apprehension. I should like to be absolutely accurate and objective, but I know that this is impossible: my original observations, or my judgement, or just simply my memory now, will let me down and prevent me from achieving my objective.

During my stay in England I took lots of notes. But now, as I look them over, I am aware that I placed too much trust then in the accuracy of my own memory, and I almost regret not having written this book entirely under my immediate impressions of that country and its people. One reason, among others, for not having done so is that I am rather mistrustful of first impressions. On making initial contact with foreign countries, especially those of superior culture, one has a certain inclination to stare in amazement or, more exactly, with some excitement, and this then leads one to look upon everything in an optimistic, even excited, way. Then, after a certain time (variable according to the temperament and the life circumstances of the observer) there ensues something of a reaction which may give an adverse slant to any judgement while it is still in the process of being formed. Each of these subjective positions can help in the maturing of a particular judgement, as long as we are able to ascertain with serenity what is due there to virtues and defects in the environment being observed and what is due to the observer's own defects and virtues. Life should be subjected to a sense of responsibility, whether at home or abroad, and, just like at home, one needs to have a normal rhythm and pattern of life, in order not to commit the injustice – whether towards our own country or towards someone else's – of judging the one or the other from too critical a perspective.

Whether these reflections were valid or not, they led me to confine my preparatory work to making quick notes, filing press clippings, organising a pile of programmes, prospectuses, advertisements and other such documents. All this material, combined with my memories and also feeding them, was meant to be the basis for composing the chapters of this book when, with my time in England already starting to seem behind me, I might have been able to look at that period in perspective and invest my words with the necessary impartiality and serenity. But I am now aware that, however close to me those days still might be, they are now retreating into the kingdom of the past – into my own past – and they are also becoming draped in a veil of that vague nostalgia which, whether happy or disagreeable, whether smiling or hateful, our past usually inspires in us. In wishing to escape from a particular cause of distortion, will I not have fallen into a different one?

*

What motivates me to write this book is, first and foremost, the pleasure of the exercise, followed by the fact that lately the attention of our intellectuals seems to be preferably attracted by England. Its language is much more studied than it used to be years ago, its literary movement is closely observed; although not yet intensively enough, translations are now appearing frequently; present-day conflicts and political developments in England are persistently talked about in our country; from time to time a great many of our major magazines and journals have devoted numbers to England's past or to its present; and finally, some of our intellectuals have spent quite long periods of residence there. This notwithstanding, England is still relatively unknown by people here. The same is true of countries which lie closer to those shores. Because of its geographical situation and its insular condition, the difficulties of its spoken language, the character itself of the inhabitants, England is still a country awaiting discovery. At the end of last century a French writer* entitled a book of hers on England *L'île inconnue*, while recently, in a lecture broadcast from London, André Maurois gave us his own account of *The Unknown Island*. If this is the experience of England's near neighbours, separated by only a narrow strip of sea which can be sailed across in an hour and a quarter, it is not surprising that Great Britain should still be the unknown island for other peoples also, or that any writer – such as myself – having seen the country with his own eyes, should believe that he has a right, almost a duty, to discover it.

There is indeed an element of discovery involved in any contact with other peoples; perhaps not so much discovering things about them as discovery of ourselves, our own individuality and the collectivity we belong to, our own nation. Chesterton** wanted to scrap in a single sentence Rudyard Kipling's affirmation along such lines. But I believe it to be beyond

---

*   Pierre de Coulevain [pseudonym of Jeanne Philomène Laperche, 1853-1927. Her journal of a sojourn in England, *L'île inconnue, moeurs anglaises*, was published in 1906].

**   *Heretics.* ['Mr Rudyard Kipling has asked in a celebrated epigram what they can know of England who know England only. It is a far deeper and sharper question to ask "What can they know of England who know only the world?"...': 'On Mr. Rudyard Kipling and Making the World Small'.]

doubt that no-one can know their own country properly if that is the only country they do know. With such a perspective they will, quite simply, have no terms of comparison on which to base their judgement. Shortcomings shared with other peoples – and perhaps imposed from outside – will look like their own exclusive defects of character, while they may well look rapturously on excellent things about themselves and their kind which are in fact part of humanity's common patrimony.

Precursory Journal Entries 1925-1926

Barcelona, 4 March 1925[1]

Estelrich[2] has proposed that I should go to Liverpool as University lector in Hispanic literatures. After some vacillation I have accepted. I shall believe it when I see it.

Palautordera[3]*, 3 May 1926*

I have received a letter from Professor Peers.[4] The trip to

---

1   The 1970 version of *Hores angleses*, in the volume *Al llarg de la meva vida* [*Throughout My Life*], did not include the two prefatory items above. Introduced there, however, were a number of previously unpublished journal entries from the period 1925–26 leading up to the author's arrival in Liverpool. These entries were incorporated by Enric Pujol as an appendix to his recent edition of Soldevila's journal (Adesiara, Barcelona 2011) as it was published in 1938. Here we reproduce selected items which shed documentary light on the circumstances of Soldevila's journey to England and on the author's state of mind in the immediately preceding period.

2   Joan Estelrich (1896–1958). Politician and writer. He was engaged in the institutional promotion of Catalan culture and occupied official positions from which he could promote internationally the Catalan case for recognition as a 'small nation' after the 1914–18 War. His activity on this front formed part of Catalan political opposition to the Spanish military government (1923–30) of Primo de Rivera.

3   The summer residence of the Soldevila family, close to the monastery of Montserrat.

4   Edgar Allison Peers (1891–52). See note 2 on page 9.

England is to go ahead. On the one hand, I find it very exciting; on the other hand, there are things – the weather, the job – which make me rather nervous.

Palautordera, 28 September 1926

We[5] leave tomorrow. I have not felt at all well for some time now. I have been working too hard recently. I have been obsessed with not falling behind in my projects here. I should have concentrated rather on building up my strength as much as possible before leaving. And I am nowhere near being in that condition. My nerves, mainly, are very fragile.

Paris, 3 October 1926

I have begun to feel better here. I like Paris very much and the climate suits me. I must arrange to come and spend a fairly long time here.

The first part of the train journey did not go well. I spent a really bad night in Toulouse, and then our next stage was on to Limoges. There we were comfortable in an attractive room, overlooking the city and the surrounding countryside. I would gladly have stayed there for longer. The rest of the journey was good. *Sylvie*, by Gérard de Nerval, was my reading: rather cloying company.

---

5   Soldevila's wife Yvonne shared with him the Liverpool experience and the English hours. Present-day readers will draw their own conclusions about the preponderance of *I* over *we* in the journal, and the fact that Yvonne is not mentioned by name until the entry for 26 January 1927.

London, 5 October 1926

By the time we reached Calais I had already the feeling of being in a new country. The *porteurs* all lined up in their uniforms to meet us, distinctly Nordic-looking types, gave me this impression. We had a good crossing and this made our arrival very agreeable, enabling me to savour every detail.

Liverpool, 13 October 1926

In my University Diary I am starting to make notes, and these, together with other observations which I shall record in this country and others which I shall not, will be the basis for writing, one day, my *Impressions of a Stay in England.*

Academic Year 1926-1927

London, 4 October 1926

When the train pulled out of Dover, dusk was falling quickly. The very fine soft mist made it harder to see the landscape clearly: there was one tunnel after another. After everything I had to listen to these last few days on the subject of the English climate and the lack of sunshine, I now had the impression that I was gradually going further and further into a smoke-filled covered space from which I would not emerge again until the spring.

At the end of a seven-hour journey, having had a quick view of London, which was crossed from one side to the other, I was agreeably surprised by the peace and quiet of a back room overlooking absolutely silent walled gardens, and then by the steady shine of the neighbourhood street-lights, harbingers of a stable life and of a compliant daily round. Soon, however, the dominant impression was another: that the silence was not a still one, between those high walls, but rather one which had a wafting motion, like a continuous, endless breath of air. A dynamic silence, I would say, despite its peacefulness and its solitude. *(On other occasions, in London, in some square with few people about, in some isolated small park, I have had the same sensation: silence, in London, has a mobile quality.)*

West Kirby, 6 October

We are now installed, the weather very overcast.

The journey between Liverpool and West Kirby, which I shall have to make regularly, seemed rather desolate. Despite the drizzle and the cold wind, one could see occasional figures walking about in the green spaces which were not built-up. At first, looking from afar, I could not understand what they were doing. Then I realised: they were playing golf.

Going from the station to our hotel we went along a deserted promenade, following the coast. The waves were breaking impetuously: just as we were about to go into the hotel, a particularly impetuous one caught us out, soaking both the taxi and our luggage.

The evening meal was rather grim: all the main dishes were served up with horrible sloppy sauces. We ate hardly anything.

7 October

It was a delight to see at such an early hour – half past eight in the morning – the hotel's big dining room full of people all nicely turned out and ready for the day's work – the men wearing smart clothes, freshly shaved, hair tidily brushed; the women, in smart clothes, attractively made-up, hair fetchingly arranged. It was a joy to see (especially after last night's fast) the tables laden with things to eat which were simple, abundant and nutritious. This was our full introduction to the English breakfast, and we did it justice. The place where we stayed in London had given us only half an introduction to it.

Afterwards I went out. My eyes were opened now to the character of English domestic architecture – typically the family house, from the relatively compact to the rather grand – of which I had only caught glimpses during the train journey. One agreeable surprise was followed by another, and my admiration grew at the same rate. Everything looked so well-tended, bright and clean, as though freshly minted: small front gardens, brick or stone-faced walls, trim white curtains to the windows, slate roofs.

Now I am sitting in the hotel lounge. All by myself. The fire is burning gently; sunlight comes through the window like a fine dust, warm and golden. Outside the sky is just faintly blue, and the sea seems enchanted by that delicate hue. A word tries to come to my lips: *happiness*. But I check it in time. It is a word to be heard, but never uttered.

8 October

'And like an echo saying "Ulysses…"' were the fitting words of the poet Rubén Darío as he surveyed the bay in Palma de Mallorca. Here, looking out on the Marine Lake formed by the Dee estuary and across to the Welsh mountains, rising up in the distance, the version would have to be: 'And like an echo saying "Tristan…"'

11 October

In class. A student says:

'I hate English history.'

And I ask: 'Aren't you English?'

'No, sir: I am Welsh.'

And the fellow student sitting next to him, also Welsh, was quick to shake the other's hand. At that point I understood why, a few minutes previously, when incidentally evoking lines of the Spanish poet Quintana on Nelson at Trafalgar, which end: *Inglés te aborrecí; héroe te admiré* – 'I hated you for being English, I admire you as a hero' – he tapped his fingers on the edge of the table, as if to show his agreement.

The other students in the class, all of them English, showed no sign at all of being riled. And this made me think of the confrontation that a small episode of this kind, so interesting in itself, would have caused in a Spanish university.

15 October

In class. I was trying to make a small change to our timetable. I tentatively suggested Wednesday afternoon. A student said:

'No classes are held on Wednesday afternoons; they are reserved for sport.'

'What about Saturday?'

'No classes on Saturdays either.'

16 October

It is strange how, when I first arrive somewhere abroad, I have a feeling of being detached and distant from everything back home. And it is strange too how soon my mind becomes steadily occupied once more by life in my own country, so that I relate to it all the things I see, everything I think about and everything I do.

17 October

I have been unable to understand properly the matter of tipping in this country. In accordance with what I once read somewhere or other, I made it my norm to give a percentage slightly above what would be usual on the Continent: my impression was that nobody took any notice. I asked around about the criterion to be followed: 'It's of no importance,' was the reply received from several people. My spirit, always inclined to see the best in everything, detected a sign of superiority in this indifference. And yet I just could not believe it. I would have liked to put it to the test by not giving any tip at all, once, only once, in order to see whether it really did not bother them. But I never found the occasion, never dared to do the bold experiment.

Finally, today, the opportunity did arise. So I put it to the test. And my conscience is still troubled with remorse about what happened. It will probably be a long time before I get over it. Even so, if there was ever an occasion when I have felt justified in letting a barber know my dissatisfaction about his work, this was most certainly it.

I was going to have my hair cut for the first time in England: the occasion did have its own importance, and its dangers. I was sitting in the chair and, while I was looking at myself in the mirror, I was forming the conclusion that will have been so often formed by men in this situation, that is to say: it is precisely when we go for a hair-cut that our hair is just at the right length and the styling just as it should be.

The art of the conscientious barber – I reflected as the hairdresser was getting things ready to attend to me – ought to conform to the following objective: that the client, on leaving the shop, should look just as though he had not been in there. Tidying up the neck, marking the hairline around the ears without making them too conspicuous, very little else… But would any barber be capable, quite of his own accord, of doing just that? He will want to do precisely the very opposite: for it to be perfectly visible that the head in question has been in his hands. Very precise orders, the strictest instructions, are called for on the part of the client, and discreet vigilance too, especially at certain crucial moments. Otherwise, one is at risk of ending up, to all intents and purposes, with a different head. Even sometimes in spite of instructions and any amount of watchfulness… A snip here, a stroke with the razor there, and the damage is done.

Did events really unfold as follows? I could not now begin to say. I did my best to explain, with words and gestures, what I wanted. I did keep an eye on what was happening. I did speak up to stay his hand. The man had no idea. The only thing he knew how to do was to cut, and keep cutting. Until finally I had to steel myself and tell him to stop. And I was left looking as bald as a coot.

If I did not then put the tipping business to the test, it would never happen. But I had to pay close attention to all the effects. They were reflected clearly enough in the face of this northern Figaro. First off there was his look of serious-ness. Then, as he realised the definitive and irrevocable nature of my abstention, his face grew longer, and paler – I do not exaggerate. While I was knotting my tie and, by watching him in the mirror, continuing my psychological scrutiny, more than once I came very close to giving in and making amends. But I did not do this: on the one hand, a kind of playful enjoyment moved me to carry the experiment through to its conclusion; on the other hand, that look of offended dignity unsettled me slightly and impelled me to bring the scene to a close as soon as possible. Still, as I was opening the door to go out (with my man already lathering the chin of another customer), I looked back to say goodbye. But that face of his… that face was truly the mask of Tragedy.

Tipping certainly can be a matter of importance!

18 October

Forebodings about the shortage of sunlight ought really to be coming true by now. However, since we arrived in England, we have had only one day without seeing the sun; and today it has shone, from dawn to dusk, in a pure, delicate, exquisite sky. Very early this morning it was already playing its games of light and shade on the curtains of our bedroom. When I was on my way into Liverpool, it was amusing itself by gently pushing the mist out towards the furthest dormitory suburbs and villages. In town it gave a sheen to the mire in the streets and it made the sky smile slightly above the dark buildings. In the evening it faded into a matt golden glow on our windowpanes. I looked out and saw it just setting behind the Welsh mountains. The waters of the estuary were tinted with the bloody red of its extinction.

30 October

NORTHERN SUN
Sunglow coming into my room,
Sunglow,
Amber your morning splendour;
Red now
In the enchanted setting
Of an iridescent evening:
Sunglow!

May your light which laughs and cries,
Your light –
Brightness, sound and warmth together,
Perfume
And blessed sweetness –
May it give fragrance to my life.
Your light!

In the eyes of my beloved,
The eyes
Where my peace has found refreshment,
- Eyes full
Of such reticent tenderness –
May there be a gleam of your light.
Lovely eyes!

In my lines inspired by time,
My poem
On delights or irritations,

Varied
Like a life in time elapsing,
May your shimmer be reflected.
My poem!

In the moment of my life's end,
Instant
Of the coffin and of the shroud,
Gliding
Beneath my eyelids when they're closed,
Please lighten the darkness for me.
Just then!

31 October

Miss W: 'The service bell is not to be rung on Sundays' (we were short of a spoon to stir our tea). It obviously accounted for why the maid, this morning, when I did ring the bell, had such a severe look on her face.

1 November

Facing the main University building, in new, purpose-built accommodation, the Students' Union is housed. When they register for their courses, all students pay a subscription of 2 pounds, 7 shillings and 6 pence, covering membership of the Guild of Undergraduates and free access to the sports fields which are three miles from the University. There are between 1,500 and 2,000 members. In the Union Building there are reading rooms, places to eat, a billiards room, etc. Many students take lunch there, where there is seating for one hundred and fifty. The sexes are separated: one wing of the building being for males, another for females, each with its own entrance. But between these two areas there is a large space in which they mingle: a hall where concerts, lectures, etc. and dances are held. There are two or three dance nights every month. The first one of each academic year is to welcome the new students. Teaching staff can also attend, and some of them actually dance – with women lecturers or even with female students.

8 November

Today, on the Mersey Railway, I saw a pregnant woman. It occurs to me that she is the first one I have seen since I came to England. And I have been here for a month now.

10 November

I have been told that burial ceremonies here do not take place until three or four days after a person has died. What a contrast with our way of doing things: scarcely twenty-four hours go by and we have already seen the back of our dead!

16 November

I find in England the same love of animals that I encountered in Switzerland. It is perhaps all the more impressive here because the people are poorer and less cultured. I recall how, during a visit to the Castilian heart of Spain, I was once told by a priest who had lived in England: 'Protestants have almost more respect for animals than for people.' And he made this affirmation in the course of a conversation on the subject of bull-fighting, which he was defending against attacks made on it by foreigners. Upon my raising the objection of finding it inconceivable that a priest could rise to the defence of such a spectacle, he told me that he was not alone in the opinion, and he invoked in his own support the authority of an illustrious Jesuit, Father Ruiz Amado, whose article on the bullfight in The *Catholic Encyclopedia* defends the activity.

I had not read the piece by the said Jesuit, but I have now been moved by curiosity to see in what terms his case was made. His arguments are deplorable, especially so being penned by a man of religion. 'Bullfights,' he says, 'have occasioned many accusations of barbarity against the Spaniards. The reason for this is, first, an utter ignorance of a contest in which man, with his intelligence and dexterity, overcomes the brutal strength and ferocity of the bull. Foreigners as a rule think that the Spanish populace go to the bullfight in order to witness the spilling of human blood. This is false. Generally, there are no casualties: and when an accident does occur, no-one derives pleasure from it; on the contrary, all deplore it. Secondly, the misconception implies a lack of comparison with other spectacles. The risks taken by acrobats, tight-rope walkers, and tamers of wild beasts are no less barbarous than those of the bullfight, although the performances themselves are less diverting. And prize-fighting is surely much more brutal, seeing that the vanquished is a human being and not a brute. Lastly, the modern theatre is frequently more reprehensible in its effects than bullfighting, which, whatever else may be said of it, arouses no immoral or anti-social passions.'

Let us ignore the poverty and the weakness of the arguments brandished by Father Ruiz Amado – the poverty and the weakness of his psychological insight. Let us observe, however, the illustrious Jesuit's neglect of the animals' suffering, probably because simple mention of this would leave his argumentation in tatters, with the cruellest consequences being for the suffering of the horses. This, in fact, is one of the most repugnant features of the Spanish national festival among all those on which foreigners' indignation is focused. This counts for nothing as far as Father Ruiz Amado is concerned. Nor does the perverse pleasure experienced by the spectators, translated into the vilest sarcasm and derision, with all the underlying hard-heartedness. This is why he can then go on to say: 'Moralists as a rule are of the opinion that bullfighting as practised in Spain is not forbidden by natural law, since the skill and dexterity of the athletes precludes immediate danger of death or of serious injury.'

In the light of these words and of the ones transcribed earlier, how can we give any credence to the following affirmation by him: 'It is false to say that the Spanish clergy encourage these spectacles'? One of the most conspicuous members of that sector is here jumping to the defence of bullfighting and subscribing to the opinion of those 'moralists' who see in it no conflict with natural law. Do not those who make such an accusation have powerful reasons for doing so? Is not the Jesuit's defence a form of encouragement?

If the Spanish clergy, or at least a section of it, thinks in this way, it is not at all surprising that very religious and strictly observant people should deem the bullfight not to be immoral and that man has the right to use animals in any way that he sees fit. I have met such people, and their very existence is proof that Catholic priests are little concerned to inculcate in their parishioners a love of animals. I have never heard a sermon on the subject of kindness to animals, nor can I recall having heard first-hand reports on that subject from any assiduous devotee of religious oratory.

Nowadays, when the name of Saint Francis is so present in the thought of many Catholics, perhaps it is the time for them to behave in such a way that his boundless love of animals enters into the hearts of the populace. Failing this, the contrast with the behaviour of the Protestant peoples will be a justified reproof of their values.

18 November

Miss P: 'Until they are seven, children have no need to be taught anything except civilised behaviour. Anything else just muddles them.'

23 November

The lector in Russian has come to my class. He recently cycled 2,000 kilometres on Spanish roads.

29 November

Miss B, who is Irish, explains how in Portugal she saw a toad which was as big as a table top. The stench it made was everywhere in the garden. In order to kill it soldiers had to be called from a nearby barracks. It took them a whole day to finish it off. In the end they blew it up with dynamite.

1 December

In class. A student – Jewish – said he felt ill. 'Last night I had no sleep, coughing all the time,' he told me. 'I think I'll go and live somewhere far away, in a southern country, in Spain. The climate here in Liverpool is horrible.' And his eyes had a glazed sheen, which could have been from lack of sleep or from feverishness.

1 December. Evening.

We went to Heswall to register with the police and to obtain our residence permit. In the mist, at dusk, across open spaces, we caught fading glimpses of houses which looked so welcoming, with their lights coming on and seeming to speak of the peace indoors amid the desolation and the sharp chill in the world outside. One has to see this sight only once in order to understand why the idea of home has such an essential importance in this country.

7 December

A journey which I do regularly from West Kirby to Liverpool. Terraced houses of Hoylake all along the railway line. Meols: a tiny, elemental station, although with added prestige from standing close to water: a pond in which stunted trees are reflected. Beyond Meols, low-lying ground with marshy patches, sad-looking meadows and rickety trees which are reminiscent of the wild olive trees in Minorca. Further away, a watchtower, grey and solitary. Moreton is where the cheap housing begins, greatly varying in dimensions, colour and category: from the sordid shack to the small, single storey detached house, simple and pretty, with its white curtains. (All these properties, in fact, have curtains: what varies is the quality, the colour and the cleanness.) Seen from the train, the overall impression is one of economic hardship or, at best, of modest comfort. P, a lecturer in the faculty, asked me some days ago:

'Would you not like to live in one of those houses?'

I responded in line with my negative impression.

'Oh, really?' he exclaimed. 'I have a friend, an established lecturer, who lives there.'

Then the flat terrain opens up more extensively, attractive to the eye, fading into the haze, especially on frosty mornings. When Bidstone junction is reached, on foggy days the fog becomes denser. You see the railway tracks disappearing into it. Locomotives come by in the other direction, puffing out thick, dirty white smoke. One has the sense of approaching a gloomy manufacturing zone. Birkenhead North. Ships' masts can be seen over the top of the railway embankment. Birkenhead Central. We change to the Mersey Railway, and go underground – and under the water of the Mersey which, for three minutes, flows above our heads. Liverpool, James Street.

London, 11 December

Few things make me sense as strongly the social vigour of England as do the British Museum and chimneys and trains puffing out smoke into the fog.

12 December

London–Dover. – In our compartment, which is full, facing one another, an Italian man and an Italian woman, who soon strike up conversation. She is magnificent, like an opulent goddess – a Juno – who might have been painted by Giorgione: regular features, clear blue eyes, a mouth which is *ampia e celeste*, fair hair characteristic of Venetians. He is a withdrawn character, very formal, dark hair with strands of silver, monocle. Conversation quickly enlivens, with a blaze that is truly meridional, these two figures who at first sight could have been taken for impassive Nordic types. They themselves have been mistaken: she took him to be North-American; he thought she was English. And it turns out that he is Genoese and lives in Vienna, while she is Venetian, living in London.

Flirtation began at once. In no time at all (she was going only as far as Dover, accompanying a silent friend who was seated beside her), he was already suggesting to her, in a persuasive tone:

'Bah! Why not continue your journey, to keep your friend company.'

Silences in the conversation were always pregnant pauses. Smiles, directly face to face, initiated by her – open, familiar, knowing smiles – immediately filled these pauses and made them more expressive than any of the words they used. Even a sustained and embarrassing faux pas, committed by him, instead of attenuating the heat of those rapid first exchanges, merely raised the level of intense scintillation.

They spoke about Italian restaurants in London. He said he preferred X to Y. She was intrigued and interested to know the reason for his preference. Perhaps this put our Genoese on his guard (Y is a restaurant which attracts its abundant clientele mainly through the lure of its private dining compartments), and he was quick to explain that the cuisine was what counted:

'Io dico per la qualità del cibo.'

The conversation then moved on in other directions, until she took out a visiting card and gave it to him.

'This man is my husband,' she said to him, then looking directly at him, in a provocative pause, almost maliciously, awaiting the result of her move.

The reaction came immediately. He shuffled abruptly in his seat and said:

'Now you have really put me on the spot. You, madame, are what the French call a *pince-sans-rire.*'

The lady was, in fact, none other than the wife of the proprietor of restaurant Y. And he went on, now as though to excuse himself – a pretty excuse since a restaurant was the case in point – saying:

'Io diceva per la qualità del cibo.'

No matter: the whole exchange was simply another pretext for them to come into greater intimacy, urgently, vehemently, enthusiastically. How Stendhal would have enjoyed this, given his love of Italy, his taste for Italian passion and sincerity, witnessing the behaviour of this couple and their vitality! Without being Stendhal, without believing that passion is the exclusive patrimony of Italy (how was he unable to find this in France itself?), without finding admirable everything that is passionate and sincere, I was delighting in all of this to the point of having to make great efforts to control my laughter, sitting there in my corner of the compartment, a comfortable spectator, watching as on either side the discreet countryside of Kent was slipping by in the delicate greyness of that morning.

Barcelona, 17 December

I have been to see Sr. Rafael Patxot:[1] 'England,' he said, 'is the only country that produces men. The rest produce machines, automatons, what you will, but not men.'

14 January

Paris–Calais. – In our compartment was a Spaniard. After we had been talking to one another for a short time, he said:

'I am from Madrid.'

'I'm from Barcelona.'

And immediately it seemed that a delicate curtain of mistrust was drawn between the two of us. There was a pause. The conversation continued, but now curiously awkward. He was the one who was having more difficulty, and before long he disappeared. We did not see him again until just as were arriving in Paris, when he came to collect his luggage.

On Dover station, however, he was walking up and down the platform, all on his own, and he must have been feeling that need for company and conversation which Castilians often feel vehemently when they are in a strange country. He came up to the window of our compartment. The restaurant service had been through serving tea and cakes: they had laid on an appetising spread for us. He cast his eyes over it, in a gaze evincing some curiosity and some despondency:

'How comfortable you are, here like this,' he said.

We invited him to join us. He did not have to be asked twice.

1   Rafael Patxot i Jubert (1872–1964): wealthy bibliophile and patron of various *catalanista* cultural projects. After the Civil War his archive was destroyed and his property confiscated by the Franco regime. He died in exile having published in 1952 his very embittered memoirs.

From that moment his reserve disappeared. He did not eat much, but he spoke a lot, despite having given the impression of not being very garrulous. He came close to being confiding, despite seeming to be a rather reserved person. When we went our separate ways, he gave me his card and said I would be welcome any time at his home.

Clearly, the fact that I was Catalan, perhaps having heard my wife and me speaking Catalan together, awoke in him that instinctive aversion that many Castilians feel towards us as a people – an aversion which, generally, disappears after a short period of being in one another's company. And his first reaction was to go with the impulse of the former sentiment. But he was unable to keep it up. The feeling of isolation and the urge to speak, and to speak in his own language, had a much stronger influence on him than any instinctive aversion.

15 January

On the way to Liverpool. – The outskirts of London; an impression of deprivation. Rectangular fields enclosed by hedges. Densely populated villages and small towns, with thousands of domestic chimneys and chimney stacks, in clusters, all smoking. Canals whose water looks stagnant; and travelling along these canals, big barges, long and narrow, fully laden, brightly painted, in procession. Undulating countryside. Very few people to be seen there, virtually nobody. Trees: firs, some poplars. Animals: white chickens, dirty-looking pigs, sheep, cows. Piles of rubbish: scrap metal, tins and cans. Tennis courts, football pitches. Haystacks. Cabbages.

West Kirby, 19 January

Everything is drying out, happily, in the sunshine. Especially the birds. One ought to be able to say exactly what these sparrows look like: chirping little sponges.

20 January

Frosty landscape. Sunshine dissolving into it.

21 January

It was snowing quite hard outside. The windows in the little library were open. The readers did not seem concerned.

23 January

This happened in the Methodist church. The collection plate was going round. I had a couple of pennies ready. And just as the plate got to me and as I was stretching out my hand to put my small contribution in it, I realised that it contained silver coins only. Too late, there was no going back. Humiliated and embarrassed, I dropped in my two pennies. And there they sat, dull, humiliated, among that abundant silver resplendence.

26 January

The day before yesterday my wife said to me:
    'There is a smell of death in this house.'
    I could smell nothing out of the ordinary. Yesterday, on returning from the University:
    'Miss R's sister is dead. She died last night.'

All the curtains had been drawn, as is the custom. After nightfall the body was collected, for it to be taken it to the church. I wanted to watch the procedure and I stationed myself by our window. It was one of those crystal-clear nights which are common here, like one gets at great height in the mountains. A van arrived. Two men came into the house carrying the coffin. Shortly afterwards they went out, with the dead body on their shoulders. They went back through the garden, through the gate in the fence, and they placed it in the van. And they departed forthwith. Nobody from the house went with them.

I expressed my wish to attend the funeral, and Miss R sent word to me that she was most grateful for this, inviting me to travel with her in the first car of the cortege.

This morning they came to collect the flowers. Yvonne was called so that she could see them before they were taken away. Then, after lunch, I was taken into the lounge, where there were even more flowers. The words of remembrance are not printed on the ribbons as in our country, but instead individually hand-written on cards by mourners in their own words. Some relatives and family friends arrived, and we set off in motor cars. One man was about to get into the one in which Miss R was to travel, and she was quick to ease him away, exclaiming:

'No: the lecturer, this seat is for the lecturer!'

The episode left me feeling ill-at-ease.

The coffin was in the Anglican church, covered with flowers. A priest appeared and read a number of psalms. The whole ceremony had a glacial coldness about it. Four men – the only ones there wearing formal clothes, dressed in morning coats and top hats – carried the coffin on their shoulders back to the hearse. A freezing wind was blowing furiously, making the naked branches of the trees sway against the back-drop of the unsettled evening sky. The freshly excavated grave was damp and deep. The casket was lowered into it with ropes. We all stepped forward to see it resting down there, getting our shoes muddied from the newly dug soil: we wanted to see how we would look eventually. The clergyman, leaning forward to where the dead woman lay, with his hand held out ready to give the blessing, read the final prayers. The wind, which was making his lined face turn livid and was blowing about grotesquely a few unruly strands of hair on his brow, snatched insistently at the pages of the holy book, interrupting the prayers and the benediction. At last, it was all over. The cleric made a rather discourteous gesture of good-bye, and we all walked away leaving the coffin exposed to the elements. Only then did I see Miss R weep, but without neglecting to express her gratitude to each and every one of us.

Back at the house an abundant buffet was laid on, with roast beef, pudding, cakes, pastries, cheese, bread and butter, tea, coffee, beer, whisky. Miss R, at one end of the table, carved the joint; at the other end another lady was pouring tea. The conversation soon became lively: people were laughing. The whole business – the feast and the conversation – seemed rather irreverent. But slowly a comfortable feeling came over me.

30 January

I went out with the intention of going to the Church of Scotland, but half way there I came across this diminutive wooden chapel. Kirby Free Church (Unitarian), the sign said. 'All seats free. All heartily welcome,' was announced below. These last words persuaded me to go in, because it is slightly intimidating to enter into such a limited circle, where everybody knows everybody else and where they ask one another who you are and what you are doing in their midst.

I pushed open the door and found myself in a room illuminated by a high central light behind frosted glass. This, together with some drapes at the far end, a small table right in the middle with a flowering plant, a couple of pianos, and the other odd detail, made it look like a photographer's studio. There were two dozen people seated on rows of chairs. The minister – a white-haired gentleman with a drooping moustache *à la gauloise*, swarthy face and vaguely Chinese eyes – was in the pulpit, a position he occupies throughout the service. He was reading a passage from the Bible: I never found out which one it was precisely. A few moments later he ended his recitation and picked up a hymn-book. We did the same. He said the number of the hymn to be sung and, from the back of the chapel, organ notes arose. Tuneful voices chimed in. These English people may not have much musical sensibility – it is rightly said – but what is also true is that their religious choirs are very pleasing to the ear. This hymn and another one which they sang – which we sang – sounded very sweetly indeed. Behind me was a young woman who sang exquisitely. Out of the corner of my eye, I caught a glimpse of her and she struck me as being very ugly. I did not try to get a better look for fear of breaking the spell. At the end of the hymn, after a short pause, the word *Amen* is spoken with infinite unction.

The minister preached a sermon recalling passages from the history of Israel and deriving lessons from the story. At the end of the sermon, we sang another hymn: 'God let thy kingdom come'. After this a young man went round with a pouch into which everybody dropped a coin or coins discreetly concealed: in this way the modesty of the offering cannot be humiliating, nor can any lavishness be ostentatious. Even so, I was able to observe that some of the faithful put in shilling coins, and one lady a note which must have been worth ten shillings, as indicated by its colour. I have been told (I do not know how reliably) that the Unitarians are few in number, but, in general, very well-to-do people. Be this as it may, it is not borne out by the simplicity, the building materials and the smallness of their temple.

After each time they have sung, the faithful bow their heads twice, but without kneeling, as the minister says a brief prayer. Throughout the service strict silence and manifest devotion are maintained.

When the worshippers left, their hands were shaken at the door, not by the minister as at the Methodist church, but by another male member of the congregation. Outside a group of young people watched me with a certain curiosity. This was the same with a young lady who was walking back in my direction, and who lives near to where we are staying. Miss N told me that Unitarians believe in Jesus, but not in his divine essence: a man of superhuman virtues, but no more than that. She also said that they have a reputation for being very good people and for doing much charitable work.

2 February

VIEW OF THE MARINE LAKE (Dee Estuary)

Breathe in, breathe in, breathe deeply
This immense peace over the sea stretching endlessly
Away to those far distant mountains.
Try to be now – now at least – like that
Light haze rising from the water, distant, slow,
Then suspended in mid-air, as if dissolving,
In the subtle sky, in the subtle, freezing light.

8 February

In class. I say:
    'Are none of you interested in political issues?'
    A student replies:
    'No, sir.'
    'What about literary subjects? Spanish literature, perhaps?'
    'No, sir.'
    'No? So why are you studying it?'
    'I don't know.'
    'What are you interested in, then?'
    'Football, card-games, chess…' And he laughed ingenuously,
without the vaguest hint of implied cynicism.

11 February

Last night the Staff Party was held in the Students' Union. The
women, with very few exceptions, were rather unattractive.
Strange really, because some very pretty ones are seen out and

about. The Head of the Italian Department introduced the two French *lectrices* to me. Two lively and agreeable young women: the type who, while perhaps enjoying themselves to a degree, exaggerate how much fun they are really having: this is self-suggestion, nothing else, which has the effect of making their enjoyment a reality for them. They poked fun at everybody.

'What amuses me most,' said one of them, an Algerian girl with slanting eyes, 'is the seriousness with which these English people dance, looking as if they are going to a funeral.'

Then an English colleague took her companion on to the dance-floor.

'Oh, *elle se tord*, what fun she is having!' she insisted to me, watching the couple move off. The truth is that there was nothing to disclose this in the face we were looking at.

The dancing involved frequent changing of partners, as I discovered when I did just once take to the floor, having to couple up with a succession of different ladies. I found out for myself that they wore very little in the way of corsetry, and that couples dance just as close together as anywhere else. When I met up again with the Algerian girl, she said:

'I danced twice with the same man, and he was obviously coming out with exactly the same words to each of his partners, because, forgetting that he had already danced with me, next time round he repeated them to me all over again.'

Walking round the rooms in the Union with the Italian lecturer, we were just about to go through a doorway when we quickly but discreetly turned tail: the charmer was heading towards us.

13 February

West Kirby Cemetery. A host of white marble crosses. Where there is no tombstone, there are marble chippings or soil, or a grass-covered mound. One grave was obviously where there had been a burial recently: the piled up flowers created an impressive sense of something broken apart, miserable. A man walked by, stood for a moment there and made a sign of acknowledgement. At another grave there were a man and a woman tidying the ground and the flowers. There was also a dog, motionless, sitting there, pensive. The inscriptions read: In affectionate remembrance… In loving memory… Sacred to the memory.

17 February

I have rented a room in Liverpool, a couple of steps from the University. It is something I want to try out. The lady of the house lavishly extolled the excellence of the accommodation – 'a very nice room' – and the 'very comfortable' quality of the house itself. When I was leaving, about to go down the stairs, she said for the twentieth time:

'Here, it is very comfortable.'

We had gone down a few steps and she insisted:

'Here, it is very comfortable.'

At the bottom of the stairs, pausing for a moment, as if she had something else to say to me, she made the point again:

'Here, it is very comfortable.'

In the hallway, heading towards the front door, she shook slightly as she gave a little laugh. And the laugh ended in:

'Here, it is very comfortable.'

And as she was closing the door, after the final 'Good-bye,

sir', she saw me off with a:

'Here, it is very comfortable.'

20 February

I got on the wrong train and instead of going to Birkenhead I went to Seacombe, I took the steam ferry to go back across the Mersey. There was a thick fog, and what was fantastic was the sound of the ships' sirens in the gloom and that of the bells on the river banks. Despite all their lights, the ships whose courses we crossed could not be seen until we were close enough to touch them. Nights like this make me understand something I heard a few days ago: that the captains of these ferries are selected from among the most expert in the profession.

22 February

I asked the Russian lector if he did not miss his own country.

'No,' he said, 'not now. At first I went through some very difficult times. The English are not very sociable. But I got married, I married here. And I shall probably spend the rest of my life here.'

And he smiled gently, torn between resignation and satisfaction.

23 February

On days like today I often recall the lines by Hilaire Belloc:

When I am living in the Midlands,
That are sodden and unkind,

I light my lamp in the evening;
My work is left behind;
And the great hills of the South Country
Come back into my mind.

The great hills of the South Country
They stand along the sea…

Except that, for me, the South Country is further south, a long way further south.

25 February

In general, continental people have mistaken ideas about the quantity and the quality of what the English eat. They arrive in England and they stay in a hotel where the only meal that they usually take is breakfast. And on the basis of this copious first meal of the day (porridge, eggs, ham, fried fish, milk, coffee, tea, bread and butter with jam) they form their judgement on all the rest.

If they were to penetrate a little further into English life, they would quickly rectify this first impression and would arrive at the conclusion that the average Englishman is rather frugal, and that the more humble sectors of English society are poorly nourished, suffering more hunger than, for example, their French or their Catalan counterparts.

The fact that their breakfast is more substantial than what we are accustomed to conforms merely to a different distribution of daily meals. It would be, however, a gross error to judge as standard the breakfasts served in hotels of the very top rankings. In family hotels like the Whitehall the menu is more or less the same, but the quantity is much less. In more modest boarding houses it is reduced to eggs and bacon with tea or coffee. And here, in this private house in Liverpool, I see a student who is lodging here swallowing every morning, deliberately and conscientiously, just a bowl of porridge: a big bowl, full to the brim, and thick porridge, certainly. But this is his main meal of the day.

Lunch is simply a small serving of meat or fish, bread and margarine, followed by some insignificant second course. And dinner is more or less the same.

Lunch, however, can be even simpler, and it often is: a sandwich, a piece of pie, what is called a quick lunch. And simpler even than this: a piece of fruit, not exclusively for vegetarians.

It is true that there is afternoon tea. But this also varies greatly: it can go from the simple infusion through to tea taken with milk, cakes or pastries, bread, butter and jam. Add to this fried fish or cold meat and take it at around six o'clock, and we have high tea, almost equivalent to an evening dinner which it even substitutes in some families. In the latter case, late in the evening, before going to bed, one has a cup of cocoa with bread and butter, or something similar. English people who take their evening meal at seven o'clock quite often have a last cup of tea at around ten o'clock.

There is too 'early tea', which does not count because it is just the beverage on its own. One takes it on waking up, while shaving, etc.

All in all, then, the food is frugal, even very frugal. As regards quality, I have observed that, in the poorer sectors of society, margarine often replaces butter; that some horrible bottled products substitute for good home-made sauces, and that tinned food, especially in modest homes, replaces steaming cooking pots and saucepans.

While frugality can be excellent for fortifying the race, I believe that an excess of frugality (involuntary for the most part, it goes without saying), poor-quality ingredients and cold meals can in the long term have deleterious effects.

'Beef and beer have made England what it is,' was the refrain, and still it is heard. But, do beef and beer sustain England nowadays?

2 March

I have heard – although I am uncertain how true it really is – that Mr. Morris, the rival of Ford and founder of the Chair of Spanish at Oxford, did not endow that post through any cultural concern or through any particular love of things Spanish, but in order to have at hand personnel with knowledge of the South American market.

Oxton – Birkenhead, 6 March

We have left West Kirby. We are now living in Birkenhead, just where the monotonous, gloomy city ends and where leafy suburbia begins. Within fifty paces the surroundings change. Trees and more trees, after so much dirty-brick high density. I push open a low wooden gate and go into one of the many private open spaces that look on to the public highway. Two rows of half a dozen houses each with its tiny front garden. Two parallel pathways which provide access and, between the paths, a lawn. Inside the house, perfect comfort. A good radio. A very select library of books in English. Looking down on the houses in front, a lot of open ground and a church steeple, severe yet paternal, designed to be seen against a backdrop of cloudy skies: its reddish matt colouring does not really go with blue skies.

7 March

We had just finished lunch when a policeman turned up. He had come to inquire why we still had not presented ourselves at the Birkenhead police station to report on our change of address. I explained that I had moved in on Saturday afternoon, that yesterday their office was closed, that this morning I had to go to the University in Liverpool, and that this evening we intended to report to the police. The explanation satisfied him: his tone suddenly changed and he struck up an agreeable conversation, recounting how he had fought in the War.

Later in the afternoon we went to the police station. They dealt with our business in a very short time. But one detail deserves comment: the policeman who was attending to us, after looking at the photograph on my residence permit, observed: 'Your hair is longer now.' (The photograph was taken around the time of the epic confrontation with that first English barber with whom I had dealings.* Some months later, after several changes of barber and much vigilance, I have been able, more or less, to put right the damage he did.)

The whole experience is indicative of the rigour and attention to detail with which police-related matters are dealt.

---

*　See the entry above for 17 October 1926.

19 March

The Easter vacation begins for me today, and I shall not have to start taking classes again until the 29th of April. I suppose that in the other English universities the holiday period between Lent Term and Summer Term will be of a similar duration, roughly. The Christmas vacation is no less generous than in Spanish universities; the Easter break is interminably longer. It is, then, a mistake to think that Spanish university life is more extravagant in its allocation of holidays than that which is usual in all the leading countries. It is likewise erroneous to believe that long periods of vacation are a waste of study time. No: the whole arrangement, neatly distributed, constitutes a harmonious whole, with the sort of harmony necessary for work in class and in preparation not to be burdensome, neither for the lecturers nor for the students. The same thing applies to the 'academic fifteen minutes'. Here in England classes occupy three quarters of an hour, on paper and in fact: in Spanish universities they are officially an hour long while lasting in fact three quarters. The truth is that anything longer than this is excessive: students' attention declines, begins to wander. Forty-five minutes is also the appropriate length of time for the person doing the teaching.

20 March

During lunch I asked Mrs. B:

'You are familiar with life on the Continent, so tell me, do people there eat more or less than people in England?'

Without hesitation she replied:

'More.'

And she added:

'People here have convinced themselves that, in order not just to live but to live well, there is no need to consume great quantities of food.'

The comparative observation is to be added to ones of this kind already made.*

22 March

To the foregoing should be added what follows:

We were talking about working-class life:

'When the men get home,' said Mrs. B, 'their wives serve them up something out of a tin. And that is their evening meal. If it were me, I would sling it back in my wife's face.'

28 March

Mrs. B explained to us that it is very normal in England, among the poorer classes, to take out life insurance, for a given sum. The proceeds of the policy, a sizeable amount of money, are to cover completely the cost of burial. A sense of pride in matters funereal is very widespread among the populace. The policies in question do give rise, however, to a horrifying distortion: some people insure newly-born infants and then let them die in order to collect the amount due. I was surprised to hear the fiercely patriotic Mrs B explaining this to us. It must be perfectly true. I consider, however, that the Englishman is marked not only by racial pride but also by a very deeply rooted class pride.

'Doctors will confirm what I am telling you,' she added.

---

*   See entries above for 17 October 1926 and 25 February 1927.

'And you will find women from the lowest strata in Birken-head who proudly tell you that they have "buried" this or that many children.'

London, 10 April

All my admiration for England will not prevent me from expressing the disappointment I have been caused here by smoke-filled theatres, cinemas, etc., reminiscent of how things were years ago back home. In trains, in trams, the English are careful about maintaining separation between smokers and non-smokers, and no-one will dare to infringe the norm. However, as the same kind of separation is impossible in places of public entertainment, the option has been taken, except in the most exclusive theatres, to give complete freedom to the smokers. In the case of such a dreadfully smoke-addicted peo-ple as the English (in university lecture-rooms they have had to display no-smoking notices), it is easy to imagine what the atmosphere there is like. The Englishman is so accustomed to smog that he feels uneasy when it is missing and he creates it by wreathing himself in smoke.

I have never been tempted by tobacco. I must confess, though, that if I have ever felt a resurgence of my adolescent fancies, it has been in England. The ubiquitous pipes here impel one to imitation. And then, if the whole truth be told, although I believe that in many respects the non-smoker has several advantages over the man who does smoke, there is one aspect in which the latter has a manifest superiority over the former. This is in conversation. And the more subtle or transcendental the talk, the more advantages are enjoyed by the smoker.

Disraeli, as an old man, racked with bronchitis, smoked during his negotiation with Bismarck. He did so, as he affirmed, because someone who is not smoking, during an important conversation, has the look of spying on his smoking interlocutor. I do not believe a word of this. The truth is that he behaved thus because, in any discussion, the person smoking can pause when it best suits him, in order to weigh his words carefully, whereas the non-smoker who attempts to do the same will inevitably give himself away.

London, 11 April

This morning, to the British Museum, Greek Antiquities department, the room displaying the Parthenon frieze. It was my whole past as a person steeped in culture, gently making its weight felt upon my spirit, swathing me in the warmest of feelings. The figures of the women in the great Panathenaic procession combined the delight of their incomparable beauty with the flow of my own memories. 'The horses of Selene, the goddess of night, pensively bow their heads': the sentence uttered by Josep Pijoan[2] was indelibly imprinted in my mind when I was studying archaeology (a subject which I failed) and it now came back to me from the distant depths of my student days. 'The richest treasure in the world,' pondered the voice of the King and chronicler Pere III,[3] down the centuries, evoking people of my own blood-line in association with the

2   Historian, poet, journalist and cultural activist, Pijoan (Barcelona 1881–Lausanne 1963) trained as an architect and taught art history in the early years of the last century, probably the phase of his career to which Soldevila alludes here.

3   The author invokes here one of the four great medieval chronicles which recount the achievements of the house of Barcelona, including Catalan expansion throughout the Mediterranean in the 14th Century.

marvellous objects which I was contemplating. I had a feeling of everything coming together, as if my own life had slipped gently along the coastlines it had followed, to arrive finally at that entrancing moment. And then some words of Leopardi were what came into my mind: '...*dal pianto / que mi sorgea sul ciglio*, the tears of lamentation that flooded into my eyes'.

London, 12 April

I went for the first time to work in the British Museum Library. An occasion which had a marvellous outcome! In order to get used to handling the catalogue, I stopped, at random, before one of the innumerable great volumes arranged in a circle around the reading room. Also at random, I opened it. And with matters still being ordained by sheer chance, my eyes fixed on a name and a title. Chance had it that these should be: Guerau de Liost, *Selvatana amor.*[4]

I smiled with delight. It seemed to me to be a propitious sign. From among the millions of books contained in the library of the British Museum, the hundreds of volumes which form the whole catalogue could have provided me with millions of titles of books from every country of the civilised world, on the most diverse and distant subjects, written in languages that were unintelligible for me. But no. I had just entered for the first time into the great rotunda, I had gone up to the catalogue, I had walked a few steps around it. And, suddenly, I had stopped in front of a particular volume (why

4   Jaume Bofill i Mates (Olot 1888–Barcelona 1933), politician and poet who used the literary pseudonym of Guerau de Liost, active in the phase of cultural nationalism in the first decades of the 20th Century. An intimate friend of Soldevila, they shared a love for the mountain district of the Montseny, where each of them had a house: Bofill in Viladrau, and Soldevila in nearby Paulautordera.

that particular one?), I had opened it randomly at a certain page (why that particular page?) and my eyes had read: Guerau de Liost, *Selvatana amor*. From among the millions of titles that the catalogue of the British Museum might have offered me, pure chance determined that I should be presented with the title of a work in Catalan, the work of a poet, a personal friend: the title of a book which evokes one of the most beautiful parts of Catalonia.

It was a dark morning. There was no fog. But there was that thick, heavy sky which seems to descend gradually over London, like a grimy canopy, until the city looks to be trapped in a dark basement. However, through that tiny printed index slip, set on its page in the big catalogue volume, through those words – Guerau de Liost, *Selvatana amor* – I had sight of a distant, shining world in its entirety: the sloping meadows; the poplar plantations; the priests taking refreshment there; the beech-woods where the hunter, early from his bed, strides purposefully; the frail and sickly woman using a parasol to help her walk and with 'a breviary as her sole companion'; the old men sitting on the stone bench, taking the winter sunshine; the mysterious water-nymphs which are the tiny fairies of the natural springs there; the valley of Viladrau and then Rosquelles, the old country home of the poet, where I had made the acquaintance of Guerau de Liost, and discovered the 'amethyst mountain' of whose charms he had sung, the countryside where I myself was made to feel I was a poet.

And into my mind there came the memory of all the yearning expressed in the exclamation in *Selvatana amor*:

O dolça vila natal,
Que vas a missa i a dansa,
quan altre record no em val,
que em valgui ta recordança!

[Oh, sweet native town, going to mass or to dance; when no other memory sustains me, may I find strength in recalling you!]

Oxford, 15 April

Nathaniel Hawthorne wrote that 'The world surely, has no other place like Oxford; it is a despair to see such a place and to have ever to leave it, for it would take a lifetime and more than one, to comprehend and enjoy it satisfactorily.'

That there is no other place in the world to compare with Oxford is, clearly, an exaggeration if by this one means that nowhere else holds so much interest. But if what Hawthorne meant was that Oxford, of its kind, has no equal (unless it be Cambridge), then a short stay in the ancient university city will convince us that his affirmation is quite true.

I had such a stay there taking advantage of a vacation period. The trouble is that it was also vacation time in Oxford, and that prevented me from enjoying the sight of the students who after dusk[5] have to wear, over their normal clothes, a special garment (a short toga or gown) wherever they go. On the other hand, I enjoyed the advantage of being able to visit more easily almost all of the colleges.

5   The original says 'until dusk falls', clearly a lapse on the author's part.

We began at random, with Balliol College. Our surprise, when we went in, was very great. The fact is that chance had taken us to one of the loveliest, oldest and most important of the Oxford colleges. Founded in 1260 by John Balliol, father of the man who was for a short time King of Scots, it is apparently among those with the most students. And the names of Robert Browning, who was an honorary fellow there and whose poems in manuscript are conserved in the library, of the economist Adam Smith, of Southey, Matthew Arnold, Swinburne and other famous men who studied there assure the eminence of its prestige.

In the main court of Balliol College I seemed to have an intuition of something which now, after three days of being in Oxford, stands out as the essence of its particular charm: in Oxford the harmonious combination of stonework, lawns and gardens attains perfection. The stones supply their severity to the combination, the grounds and gardens their sweet softness. I know of no other place where both qualities, apparently conflicting, are merged with such penetrating intimacy. And I would go as far as to say that both parties are active in this rapport: the stones often taking on greenish-ochre hues, as though in transition to a plant-like condition; while the plant growth, running out into ivy and Virginia creepers, clings to the masonry as though to adopt its shape. And if this shape is sometimes emphasised by the horticultural features which frame a building, at other times it is the building which frames the garden, accentuating its green peacefulness. Selecting a perspective on the lawns and flower borders which are framed through main gates and other doorways, through windows, through arcading in cloisters; pausing for a while, inside any one such setting, savouring slowly the peace and the perfume: these are two of the finest delights which Oxford has to offer.

In this regard, besides Balliol, also admirable are New College, Worcester, Magdalen, Wadham. But, for all the wonders of New College gardens in their castellated precincts, or of the grounds of Magdalen College, divided by an arm of the River Cherwell, those of Wadham College would be, I think, my favourites. The lawns and the flowerbeds stretch out before the polychrome walls of the Gothic chapel – ochre, sepia, green – a delicate seventeenth century construction which one would unhesitatingly ascribe to the fifteenth century. Constant birdsong comes from the trees. The chiming of all the hours is carried into this well-tended arbour as though the sounds of so many different bells were converging there by appointment; and one's ear picks up the noises of the city, muffled but loud enough for the contrast to be made.

The peace and quiet in these gardens does not arise from their remoteness. They are inside Oxford itself, and Oxford is a living, bustling city. If it does have back-streets where life seems to have stood still, as though in ecstasy, its thoroughfares are thronged, at times almost throbbing, with people and traffic. To know that noise and commotion are close at hand while one is enjoying peacefulness is, perhaps, the best kind of peace. And it is this which one feels in the divine gardens of Wadham College.

There are some colleges which do not have gardens, but these are very much the exception. Most do have, at least, lawns in the middle of their quadrangles or cloisters. This is enough to soften their severity. The effects achieved by this combination are surprising. On the other hand, the colleges with no greenery at all have a dry, coriaceous harshness. They have an oppressive effect on your state of mind. And if such a thing happens at this time of year, what must it be like in autumn or in winter, when they are shrouded in mist? The mere thought of this seems to make clear to me the intimate meaning of an epitaph from 1639 in Christ Church Cathedral which reads:

> *Paucis notus, paucioribus ignotus,*
> *hic jacet*
> *Democritus, junior,*
> *cui vitam dedit et mortem*
> *Melancholia.* *

In general, however, the sensation created by Oxford is that of equilibrium: the balance between severity and soft-ness, between tradition and modernity, between the quest for knowledge and sporting activity, even between the sadness of grey days and the splendour of fine weather, because if this region is especially favoured by mists, the Oxfordshire spring is, on the other hand, famous. And this complete equilibrium could explain Oxford's efficiency in forming the ruling classes of England.

16 April

Warwick. Of all the towns and villages of 'Shakespeare country', none – if we except Stratford, where the great poet was born and died – is as important as Warwick. The famous castle, Saint

---

* Known by few, unknown by fewer, / here lies / Democritus junior / to whom life, and death, were given / by Melancoly.

Mary's church, the Lord Leycester Hospital, the East and West gates, many ancient houses which retain their medieval aspect: all of these make Warwick one of the most interesting historic towns in England. The castle, above all, is the objective for us of an assiduous pilgrimage.

Situated at one extreme of the town, set in marvellous parkland, standing over the leafy banks of the River Avon, its majesty and its charm are supplied at least as much by the vegetation and the waters which surround it as by its own qualities, its own lines and colouration.

Access is gained along a narrow avenue which is overhung, in this spring weather, by a dense canopy of green. At a bend in the pathway there arises before your eyes a tower which is both sturdy and slender, standing out white among the great trees: this is Caesar's Tower, the oldest remaining part of the present building, 150 feet high, constructed, it seems, shortly after the Norman Conquest.

We walk slowly up the short ramp which leads us to the big double gate, flanked by turrets and draped with ivy. Through it we go, to find ourselves suddenly in the inner courtyard of the castle. If previously we had gone along filled with admiration, our sense of wonder is now heightened further. What a delight this courtyard is! Enclosed by walls, flanked by towers; yet no-one setting foot inside there would dare imagine the clangour of arms or loud warlike cries. Warwick Castle, reckoned to be the most picturesque feudal residence in all England, here has nothing warlike about it: it is simply idyllic. And this idyllic quality has simply nothing ancient about it, neither medieval nor even eighteenth century; it is, rather, of our own time, of the here and now. We would need to make a considerable mental effort for love stories of centuries long since past to be evoked for us by this vast and fragrant expanse of lawn, by these pathways surrounding it, by this more modern assemblage of buildings constituting almost more a palace than a castle, by even these towers and walls which seen from within are far from imposing. By contrast, and quite naturally, effortlessly, there drifts into our minds the image of a modern-day young woman, one of the 'bright young things', that rare mix of elegance and vigour, in simple spring clothes, with an extremely short skirt complementing perfect legs; and, at her side, a dapper young man with parted hair (in England the parting is still the almost absolute king of hairstyles), impeccably dressed, with such an intelligent and charming air that one can only believe the 'distinguished sportsman' look, so grotesquely abused in our country, to be indeed a true flower of civilisation.

Having left one group of visitors and getting ready to begin his work again with the people waiting to be shown round the interior, the castle guide dispels our simple evocative train of thought and replaces it with his commentary, which he delivers with a smugness disguised as cheerful bonhomie. We go through rooms full of paintings and tapestries, sumptuously furnished, all of them with views over the river. This castle houses certainly one of the finest collections of Van Dycks; works by Rubens abound; there is a splendid assemblage of opulent suits of armour: the famous Warwick Vase, discovered at the Tiburtine Villa of the Emperor Hadrian, in Tivoli, and acquired by Sir William Hamilton, takes its name from this castle where it is kept.

Within these sumptuous rooms, the idyllic feeling which we had outside is now stifled by their very sumptuousness, by a certain coldness that one feels in a museum, and by the vague anxiety attaching to sinister historical memories. Even the landscape, viewed through these windows – with the thick woodland and with the River Avon sliding by, deep, narrow and greenish – has a beauty which is slightly solemn. And seen from the ground floor level, on this side of the building, the castle's superb bulk stretches away, with its Gothic high windows and its battlements, its towers and turrets, with the robust foundations which the river laps up against and which are adorned with wild plants. It was surely in recalling this aspect of the castle that Hawthorne wrote: 'We can scarcely think the scene real, so completely do the machicolated towers, the long line of battlements, the massive buttresses, the high-windowed walls, shape out our indistinct ideas of the antique time.'

The 'indistinct ideas' which this view of the castle succeeds in giving shape to are, we might say, those suggested by a passage from Tennyson: 'night, the dark boat drawing close to the castle, decked out in funeral drapes which trail on the waters; the boatman seated silently at the prow; and, deathly pale in moonlight, the exquisite maiden lying as though asleep, a faint smile on her lips, the lily in her right hand, and the letter – the fateful letter – in her left hand.'

Thus the castle steadily reveals its secrets to us, and we have no difficulty in understanding that character of Dickens – Feenix – in *Dombey and Son*. Do you recall the words which Mrs. Skewton says to the reader about him; 'He has been to Warwick Castle fifty times, if he has been there once; yet if he came to Leamington tomorrow – I wish he would, dear angel! – he would make his fifty-second visit next day.'

Nor, for sure, would he neglect to go to Saint Mary's church, to view there the noble tombs of the Counts of Warwick and of Leicester, to contemplate its singular bell tower and to go into ecstasy at the sound of the bells, which make the hours float across the roof-tops of Warwick with a sequence of ingenuous peals.

Stratford, 18 April

Upon a plain, criss-crossed by low ridges, among orchards and meadows, stands the town where Shakespeare was born and where he died: Stratford-on-Avon.

It is a municipality of around ten thousand inhabitants, the streets of which are wide and clean, seemingly completely modern were it not for the half-timbered houses which we find there at intervals.

We arrived yesterday. Already beginning are the festivities organised there annually to commemorate the date of the poet's birth (April 23, 1564): a civic parade and a sequence of performances of his works constitute the main part of the festival programme, which lasts for almost a month.

The weather today has been prematurely and ephemerally warm. English spring was bursting out, shining and opulent. All the trees are in blossom. Noisy, cheerful people thronged the streets, restaurants and the banks of the river, resting or disporting themselves on the grass, as if at a *fête champêtre*, watching the slender, shiny boats scudding in both directions on the water. Making it difficult to indulge in private contemplation, the same crowds also filled the places which hold particular historic associations with the life of the great dramatist: the house where he was born, with its small rooms, their low ceilings and greyish walls, some of these still showing the names of many visitors, among which one can still read those of Walter Scott, Carlyle, Thackeray, Kean, Browning; the garden attached to the property containing a selection of trees and flowers mentioned by Shakespeare in his works; the small museum at New Place, close to the site of the house where he lived on his return to Stratford; the grammar school where he studied as a boy; Holy Trinity church, already on the attractive edge of the old town, close to the river – a lovely Gothic temple where his tomb is located, together with those of his wife and daughter. There too on the chancel wall is the funerary bust, sculpted shortly after the poet's death by Gerard Johnson. One would rather it were not on view there. Looking at it, as when looking at the portrait which figures in the 1623 First Folio edition, I was made to think once again that Shakespeare has been one of the most unfortunate of geniuses as regards his effigy: the only two likenesses which, despite the differences between them, offer any guarantee of authenticity show him as rather dim-looking, and both works are appallingly mediocre.

In the evening, a production of *The Taming of the Shrew*, with a splendid Petruchio, vibrant and godlike; a ravishingly beautiful and gloriously ferocious Katherine; and with some embellishments on Shakespeare's text, scenically most effective it must be said. Thus at the end of act one, scene two, when he is forcibly carrying Katherine to the nuptial chamber, she resists while protesting, ever less energetically and more despairingly, 'I will my supper, I will my supper.' Likewise, at the end of another scene in the same act, there is an innovation-which could – or does – come straight from the end of the first act of *Mar i cel*.[6] Katherine draws a dagger in order to repulse Petruchio. He, on seeing this, instead of resisting, presents his chest to the thrust. She drops the dagger and bursts into tears. All this is pure Guimerà. The only difference is that the Catalan dramatist makes his female protagonist fall into a faint.

19 April

Not all Shakespearian memories are sited in Stratford. Early this morning we went to Anne Hathaway's cottage, the childhood home of the poet's wife. The crowds had melted away and a delicate, pinkish mist was hanging over the empty fields. The car glided smoothly along the lead-coloured road surface. How frequently must Shakespeare have made his way across the same fields, going by night to the secluded home of his beloved, or returning from there at first light, after the hours of making love! As one stands before this humble thatched cottage, which retains both outside and inside all the character of another age, the memory of the poet surges forth more vividly than anywhere in Stratford itself: more than when one looks at his birthplace, or at the school where he studied, or when one stands before his tomb itself.

Here we see him in the first flush of youth, bold, passionate and overflowing with the life which will pour forth abundantly in his works. Here is where he comes at night, a youth of seventeen; he climbs up to this small window of the room where he encounters Anne in the fullness of her womanhood (she was eight years older than him) who holds him all night

6   *Mar i cel* (*Sea and Sky*, 1888) a play by the celebrated Catalan dramatist Àngel Guimerà (1845–1924). Soldevila's comparison here is obviously whimsical and fanciful, perhaps inspired as a tribute to Guimerà by memory of the author's relatively recent death.

in her arms and who has no illusions about the brightness of dawn nor the song of the lark. Every night the nightingale trills in that part of the garden… The separation of Romeo and Juliet was evoked for me last evening by the endless song of nightingales intoxicated with emotion. The sound reached me, together with the scent of pear-blossom, through the high window of my room, and now the vision of the lovers has come back again, even more powerfully, inside Anne Hathaway's cottage.

Something which was also readily evoked there was Shakespeare in his old age. His pleasure, after retirement to his native town, was to go regularly and often to the cottage, to spend long hours there: in the garden in summer, by that same fireside in winter. He could have applied to himself the words he puts into the mouth of the Earl of Worcester, in *Henry IV*, Part 1:

> For mine own part, I could be well content
> To entertain the lag-end of my life
> With quiet hours.

I believe that this desire and this hope, sharpened by the memory of his home town, such a haven of tranquillity, must have contributed greatly to preventing Shakespeare from being engulfed in the maelstrom of his own genius and his life as an actor in the bohemian milieu of the Elizabethan age. Penury, debauchery, ambivalent love affairs, an inquisitive absorption in the depths of his own inner life and the inner lives of others, all such things could be and were transcended through his powerful vitality. The hope or, rather, the certainty of respite available in that place far from London, among the orchards and meadows, in the company of his wife and his daughters, among his old friends, must have provided him with reassuring support. Is it not true that, eleven years after he left Stratford, having amassed a not inconsiderable fortune (a practical instinct, saving and speculating, which must also have contributed to his survival), we find him spending periods of time in his home town, purchasing the finest of houses there, with a garden and farmland? Do we not find him gradually expanding his estate?

The countryman in Shakespeare must not be overlooked if we are to understand him properly. Acquaintance with his home town can help us greatly in this.

29 April

First day of classes after the Easter vacation. The students have possibly read a book or two during this period, but they have done no preparation, absolutely none. All of them have come back looking healthier. Instead of getting angry, I could not refrain from complimenting them on this – sincerely.

2 May

If the statistics are to be believed, English trains achieve the fastest speeds in the world. They are comfortable, luxurious: third-class accommodation on one of the main English lines is as good as and even superior, in that regard, to first-class on express services in Spain. It has to be said, though, that there is the disadvantage of twelve people, if necessary, having to squeeze into each compartment, in which case things are rather cramped. The main drawback here is the cost of tickets, almost equivalent to our first-class fares. Despite the higher level of wages, poor people in England must have difficulty in affording journeys of any considerable length, and, in fact, it is very unusual to share a compartment with folk of humble condition. Almost everybody travels third-class: there is no second-class accommodation (except between London and the Channel ports); and the only people who use first-class are aristocrats, captains of industry, senior businessmen, and academics who receive 'five guineas and first-class expenses', the usual remuneration for giving an invited lecture.

14 May

I have been wondering lately when the swallows would arrive. This morning their screeching announced that they were here. 'Swallows!' I said to Yvonne, as I rushed to the window to see them.

15 June

On the train, heading for Edinburgh. After Oxenholme, hills: few trees, but grass on the slopes gives them a soft appearance. The river looks less and less like a typical English one, not now like a canal, flowing between tight banks, but meandering freely over the stones visible on the bottom. Yellow marigolds, sparse trees, stone-built houses – brick not now much in evidence – with slate roofs. Here and there darker patches of grass show on the hill-sides; some scattered boulders are hard to distinguish from the motionless shaggy sheep: now the landscape becomes harsh. Broom in flower. Few villages. Farmsteads. We can make out the first high mountains: patches of woodland.

Deeper into Scotland: hills, hills, and more hills. Cows. A rabbit scurries away as the train goes by. A scarecrow flutters. Big expanses of firs, while here and there a different tree, light green, appears more frequently. When the vista opens up, pale hues (green, amethyst) are seen on the mountains in the distance. A golf course: pale young women stand out against the green backdrop. I become aware that one sees here fewer sports fields than in England.

Edinburgh, 16 June

Coming here from the English cities, with their buildings of brick blackened by smog and smoke – London or Birmingham, Liverpool or Manchester – the capital of Scotland surprises and straight away captivates you. Stone, noble ashlar masonry, has replaced brick, the smoke has disappeared, and the mist untainted by smoke has become a winged apparition in suspension between water and sky, veiling and blurring the surroundings, quite unlike that heavy phantom presence which seems to ooze from the dirt, concealing and oppressing. Then there is the contact with the countryside: you have the sense of this proximity even in the very centre of the city. This contrasts sharply with the feeling one has in the vast English cities, despite all their urban squares and parks full of trees. And if you do find there anything like a similar closeness to nature, it is merely as a kind of aspiration capable of creating a particularly tender mood: Virginia creepers whose colours indicate the passing of the seasons, clinging to the dark walls of a house; ivy which drapes a fence; plant pots, a flowerbed lamenting times past.

The main thoroughfare in Edinburgh, Princes Street, considered to be one of the finest in Europe (the very finest, as some claim?) has tall, well constructed houses along one side, but on all the other side there is not a single construction except the great monument to Walter Scott: gardens occupy the rest of that expanse. And beyond the gardens and the railway line there are steeply sloping green banks above which the old city seems to rise. Looking to the right and to the left, limiting the view at either end of Princes Street, one sees the high ground on which stand the Castle and the old Observatory. This, precisely, forms the magnificent panorama of Edinburgh, a setting which is not laid out around the city, as in certain places with which comparison might be made (Barcelona or Liverpool, for example), but which constitutes rather the very heart of the place. And the Castle, that severe Acropolis, standing proudly upon its craggy hill top, dominating the neoclassical buildings at its feet (the Royal Institution and the National Gallery) fully justify the name of 'Athens of the North' given to the Scottish capital.

The marvellous coming together of nature and art is set in relief by history. Memories of old Scotland abound in the Castle, in Saint Giles's church, in Parliament House, in the home of John Knox. But where we are most intimately wrapped in these memories is in Holyrood Palace. This building, occupying the site of Holyrood Abbey, founded in 1128 by David I, the only remains of which – a model of historical ruins scrupulously conserved – are today what is left of the nave. This was the original residence of the kings of Scotland. But what we see nowadays dates from 1670–1679. It is an enormous building at the eastern extreme of the city, its pointed towers dominating the horizon from the stark, rocky elevation where it stands. The whole complex has a sad hardness about it. Is this because of the tragic atmosphere it exhales?

The kind of bloodstained nightmare which constitutes one of the most shocking aspects of the history of England is to be encountered inside the silent rooms of the palace of the kings of Scotland. It is condensed, above all, in a single name: that of a passionate and ill-fated young woman: Mary Stuart, Queen of Scots. Here, in this little room next to the royal chamber, on the night of March 9, 1566 the Queen was dining in the company of her secretary and favourite, the Italian David Rizzio, and other people from her intimate circle. Now and again, a lady would disappear for a moment into a tiny closet (so cramped it could have been taken rather for a wardrobe) to emerge with her make-up refreshed. All of a sudden, the door of the royal chamber was violently thrown open. A number of men threw themselves upon Rizzio, who was just able to cling to the Queen's dress. But she herself was roughly overpowered. Who was the senseless individual who dared to lay hand on the queen? It was her husband, Lord Darnley. While he himself was restraining the royal personage, Rizzio was dragged away through the palace chambers and finally left in the vestibule to the audience hall, his body pierced by fifty-six stab wounds. To this day a copper plaque marks the place where he was left by his assassins.

In the same room, by one of the windows, there is a facsimile of the letter addressed by the unfortunate queen, the day before her execution, to the king of France – the same France where her happiest days had been spent, where she had been adored by a king and his court and where a great poet, Ronsard, had been her poetry tutor. The contrast brings to mind another phase of her misfortune: her nineteen years of captivity under the power of Elizabeth of England, her enforced pilgrimage from one prison to the next, from Bolton Castle to Tutbury, from Tutbury to Wingfield, to Coventry, to Chatsworth, to Sheffield, to Buxton, to Chartley, to Fotheringhay; the decline in her beauty and her health; the intrigues of Catholics all across Europe (England, France, Spain, Italy) to save her and to put her in the place of her rival for the crown of England; the execution of the Duke of Norfolk, to whom Mary had promised her hand in marriage if he succeeded in procuring her release. Finally, the tragic denouement, with her refusal to accept the priest of the hated religion they wanted to impose on her; with the heart-rending cry 'Into thy hands, O Lord, I commend my spirit'; with the three axe-blows delivered on that delicate neck which seemed to resist the separation of her head and body.

*

There is nothing better – in order to repel, to finally obliterate, all these sinister memories – than a tour of the outskirts of Edinburgh, to Portobello or to the Forth Bridge, following the wide thoroughfares flanked by dripping trees. The Forth Bridge, in particular, an immense iron construction joining the two banks of the Forth, is well worth a visit. This is so on account of the route which leads there, the site where it stands so proud, and its imposing massive presence which does not lack elegance and which (curiously) does not intrude on the surrounding countryside: a mountain would not look better there. The small village of South Queensferry cowers, with its tiny houses, almost directly beneath it. The river's waters are flat and still, like those of a lake, silver-coloured and giving off a strong smell of salt. A majestic silence reigns, faintly broken, all of a sudden, by a distant sound of iron against iron. The noise comes nearer, louder, spreading upwards in the air. You notice that a train, as small as a toy, is moving smoothly, urgently across the high span. Momentarily you fear for its safety. But it goes, decisively, over the exposed central stretch of the bridge. Then onwards it travels again across dry land. Its noise fades away. And the majestic silence once more is all around. And you feel first the prick and then the welling up inside you of a sense of distance.

In the city, this same feeling often affects you, more, much more than in any English city, even though Edinburgh in its external appearance is more like its continental counterparts. There is something, something beyond geographical aware-ness, which makes us feel all the distance separating us from our true selves: something in the clarity of bright days and in the greyness of foggy days, in the simplicity and monotony of colour combinations in the spreading countryside and rolling hills, in the Highlanders' many-coloured dress, in the melancholic music of their bagpipes, in the blueness of young women's eyes.

A sort of gentle sweetness dominates the feeling of being so far away from your own latitudes: a sort of sweetness which is the inversion of nostalgia or home-sickness.

Glasgow, 17 June

On arrival at the hotel I was presented with the guest book. Reading what I had written there, the lady in the reception office put on a rather cross face and said, pushing a different book towards me:

'Ah! So you are a foreigner? You should have written in this book, not in that one.'

'I wrote in the book you gave me, madam.'

How the devil, with my accent and my appearance, can they think I am British? Be it as it may, I reckon that our opening exchange prejudiced the good woman against me, but perhaps that is how she was with everybody. And the incident did prejudice me against her. Did not somebody once speak to me about the dourness of the Scots? I think so. But were it not for that woman, I would not have remembered.

I went out. Glasgow struck me as being a monotonous and disordered city. The streets along which I went displayed nothing of particular note. Except for the University, standing tall, overlooking parkland on every side, the buildings brightened by the afternoon sunshine – a benevolent sunlight, damp and slightly discoloured by recent showers.

In the company of GL, who came over from Edinburgh, I went to see Professor E. We met him, sitting in a park near to his house, taking the sun and reading. When I told him that I had come from Edinburgh and that tomorrow I planned to leave for the English Lake District, he replied, quite surprised and as if somewhat vexed:

'And what about the Scottish Lakes?'

The Trossachs, 18 June

The Scottish Lakes. – Less well known and less renowned than the English Lakes (even far less than those of Switzerland, Italy and the Savoy), the lakes of Scotland are every bit as worthy of being known about and visited. Here is where the Scottish landscape is displayed in all its mysterious beauty.

I confess that going through southern Scotland, between Carlisle and Edinburgh and then from Edinburgh to Glasgow – with the exception of the capital and its surroundings – I felt rather disappointed. The weather was no doubt a factor in this: soft landscapes require a filter of dampness in the air – the sky might be clear or cloudy, but there must be some humidity. And quite by exceptional chance we encountered weather which could almost be called hot, with a lowering quality in the atmosphere.

On the other hand, the literary prestige of Scotland's landscape is so great that one's expectations about it will not be easily fulfilled. However, from the moment that this morning we embarked at Balloch on one of the little steam ferries that ply between one end and the other of Loch Lomond, the biggest and perhaps the loveliest of the Scottish lakes, my own expectation was satisfied: it was also considerably modified. Dark waters and light green woods dropping down from the hillsides to the very edge of the lake; small islands here and there dotting the surface with clumps of vegetation; occasional tiny villages by the shore, with single-storey houses made of neat stone blocks, slate roofs, nestling between the hills and the lake; the whole imposing backdrop of high mountains crowded together and blocking the northern end of the valley; and, over the whole scene, a changing, unsettled sky which was filled at one moment with dense storm clouds and at the next with sparkling limpidity: this was the view of Loch Lomond which we enjoyed today.

To the comfortable feeling of the boat slipping weightlessly across the water and the vista itself were added numerous pleasant details: young men proudly displaying the traditional Scottish dress; the infectiously melancholy sound of the bagpipes; literary reminiscences of Walter Scott; tents on the banks of the loch; girls on a hilltop there, waving handkerchiefs to greet a troop of friends arriving on our boat; and, in particular, a small choral group singing, throughout the crossing, popular Scottish songs.

Men and women, they were singing with smiles on their lips, with the visible satisfaction of performing a joyful patriotic ritual. The smiles became sad ones at times, because not everything can be gaiety in the songs of a country which has been violently subjected to the power of another. Around the choir, people were gathered, listening thoughtfully and following with devotion the words and the rhythms of the songs. There was one which was especially moving: it spoke of Scotland's hills, its vales and dales ('Scotland's hills for me' was the refrain), of the fields where battle had been done by Wallace (the ill-fated hero of Scottish independence), and the words 'Scotland yet' returned again and again like the sigh of a hopeful yet timorous aspiration. The faces of the singers and of those listening reflected their deep emotion. I do not think that I was the person least stirred by it all.

After the songs there came the dances. Some lads began the session at the far end of the boat, to the accordion-like sound of harmonicas. For a short time they were all holding hands, doing a set of steps similar to those of our *sardana*;[7] then suddenly they performed a sequence of figures accompanied, every now and then, by leaps and shrill cries. After this two couples did a different dance, either with arms around their partners or else holding hands, stamping their feet vigorously and, just the women, emitting the same shrill scream, guttural and trembling.

Meanwhile our steamer had travelled almost the full length of the loch, moving ever nearer to where the interlocking bulks of the mountains closed in on the head of the valley. At Inversnaid we disembarked and were met by one of those large old-fashioned carriages, drawn by four horses, with the coachman wearing a red dress-coat and a grey top hat. You might say it was a bit of show for the benefit of the tourists. No doubt it was: a motor coach would have covered much more quickly the five miles which separate Loch Lomond from Loch Katrine. But staged effects of this kind are basically authentic, and the traveller who has any feeling for the past cannot but appreciate them. So we happily mount the steps and take our seats; the horses begin to trot, and before long there we are, in the heart of the kingdom of Rob Roy and the Lady of the Lake.

We go gradually uphill, leaving behind the thick ash-woods. Bracken and heather soon become the predominant, almost exclusive, vegetation. Our lungs are filled with their cool scents, and we feel the sense of freedom one has when close to the mountain tops. The peaks rise up on both sides of

---

7   The *Sardana* became the national dance of Catalonia towards the end of the nineteenth century. It is performed in public spaces to music played on traditional wind-instruments. Circles of people, with their hands joined and raised, dance with very precise steps to a quite complex pattern of figures. The circles grow in size as more dancers join in.

the route, which is soon passing along the edge of the small Loch Arklet. The mist breaks up in wisps around the summits. Waterfalls tumble down from them, with the appearance, seen from afar, of ribbons of snow left behind in the gullies. Sheep graze everywhere, roaming freely in ones and twos. The cold wind ruffles their long, unshorn fleeces. Suddenly there is a small break in the horizon and we have a view in front of us of Loch Katrine, much smaller than Loch Lomond, but no less attractive. On the other hand it is set in a wilder landscape, preserving more intact the poetry and the mystery suffused there. In this respect the Scottish lakes have the advantage over their better known Swiss counterparts. It is undeniable that the Highlands have been fortunate in having two great poets – Walter Scott and Robert Burns – who not only picked up a whole poetic tradition and its associations with this landscape, but who also enhanced it with the grandeur of their inspiration. Thus, although you might not be well acquainted with their actual writings, their presence accompanies you throughout the tour we are now on. Loch Katrine (the location of *Lady of the Lake*), Loch Achray (the tiny enchanted lake of the Trossachs) both are pregnant with the mood of Scott's poem. And everything here – lochs and rushing streams, glens and mountain tops – reminds you of lines by Burns, in particular those of the famous poem which begins:

My heart's in the Highlands, my heart is not here;
My heart's in the Highlands, a-chasing the deer...

*

Evening is falling now, as the white night of these northern skies approaches, close by Loch Achray, a lake of one's dreams, set in a narrow valley. From my bed I can see it between a tower of our hotel-cum-castle and the abundant mountain greenery. It is quite silver, seen as a broad rippling band close to one shore, gradually merging into the still, deep shade on the other side. But slowly the silver colour advances. In the background a mountain rises high, sharply outlined, with typical green patches, a smudge of dark cloud over its summit, and then the clear, pearl-coloured sky. A single sound is heard, the monotonous, melancholy call of a bird. Which kind of bird? I do not know, nor do I need to know.

Academic Year 1927-1928

4 October, 1927

Calais-Dover. – A motionless and oily sea, running from the west. Reddish sails. An aeroplane above the packet boat. (Copulation of iron with iron?)

London. – Thick fog: the station lights hang from the firmament.

Oxton, 5 October

A good journey, a bright day, the decorum of Cheshire. Arrival at Oxton.

11 October

The habit of stretching to shake off drowsiness is obviously widespread in this country. Students of both sexes (even with bare arms, showing their armpits) stretch their limbs in the library and they sometimes even do so – very occasionally – in class. I have raised this matter with them: 'In the company of classmates…,' has been the response. But I do not think that it happens only in this circumstance. And, even so…

12 October

A speech by Lord Cecil. – In his crusade through England, preaching in favour of the enhancement of the League of Nations' role, propounding an ideal of world peace, and attempting to justify his withdrawal from the Geneva talks, Lord Robert Cecil visited Liverpool. He made two speeches: one of them addressed to the League of Nations Association, another one especially for the students.

I have noted the interest shown by English students in the international organisation based in Geneva and the existence of university societies supporting the League of Nations, together forming the British Universities League of Nations Society. Lord Cecil, demonstrating his commitment to the movement, gave one of his speeches to the Liverpool University group.

In fact, Lord Cecil said nothing that he has not expressed in other speeches or in more widely publicised declarations. What has to be emphasised, however, because it is always worth stressing this, is his insistence on the possibility of reaching a peaceful solution to contention between nations, in the same way that peaceful judicial solutions have been achieved for individual disputes; his insistence on the need for disarmament as the first step towards this, and his declaration that France must be given sufficient guarantees of security for it to be freed from suspicion and from fear of being invaded again.

But what I want above all to put on record is the atmosphere of the meeting. Gilmour Hall, where the Students' Union is housed, was filled with students, the males on one side and females on the other. The chairs were arranged in such a way that the two contingents were seated not side by side, but facing one another. And it was pleasing to see those two groups of young people listening to and (stamping their feet as well as, or even more than, just clapping) showing their approval of the venerable old man, so elegantly noble-hearted, who was speaking to them about peace and about concord among peoples. Seeing him with his white hair (which forms a kind of halo at the back of his head and which was lit up by the dingy sunlight coming in through the high windows); with his hook nose upon which, in a gesture which must be second nature to him, every now and then he would crook his index finger; with his small, grey eyes, rather dimmed as though by a veil which does not quite conceal their intelligent vivacity; with his great height, now slightly stooping; with sober gestures used sparingly just to underline some key passage, we were reminded of that striking caricature reproduced in *La Publictat*.[8] It shows the Society of Nations represented by a young woman in tears, with Lord Cecil embracing her, paternally, and saying to her: 'You are still young, and other men will break your heart.'

The mutual understanding between the speaker and his audience became even stronger when, once the lecture was concluded, the students began to address questions to Lord Cecil about his subject. 'That is a very interesting point,' he would say with emphasis, rising once more to his feet to respond to an intervention; or, 'This is a difficult question

8   We may speculate that the caricature referred to here is probably a reproduction of a contemporary English cartoon from a journal such as *Punch*.

to answer,' said slowly as he rubbed his nose, looking very thoughtful. 'What can be done by me and my fellow country-men who share the same high ideals,' asked a German student, 'what can be done to send to Geneva a man who truly repre-sents us, rather than Herr Stresseman, who is a militarist deep down?' 'Every country,' responded Lord Cecil, 'must strive to find representatives that truly embody its values.' 'Should not measures be taken to prevent the showing of films where scenes of war appear and which foster bellicose instincts?' 'The war films which I have seen,' replied Lord Cecil, 'did not strike me as being capable of having that kind of effect but rather, on the contrary, of arousing indignation, pity, repugnance, the desire to put an end to so much barbarism.' 'What can be done,' a lecturer asked, 'to stop overpopulation from taking men off to war?' 'I do not believe that, at the present moment, humanity can invoke overpopulation as an excuse for waging war. Two hundred years from now it could be a different question,' was Lord Cecil's reply.

And in this way the questions and answers (the latter summarised schematically by me, and which in some cases became short speeches in themselves) followed one upon the other, most attentively listened to by the whole gathering. It was an impressive performance, lasting for almost an hour. Finally the chairman had to bring proceedings to a close in order to call for the vote of thanks to be given by Professor Peter Roxby, president of the university branch of the Association. He observed how appropriate it was that Lord Cecil should have begun in Liverpool his promotional campaign among students, as the University here had been the first one to found an Asso-ciation promoting the cause of the League of Nations.

Finally the president of the Students' Union thanked Lord Cecil again and then closed the meeting with the ritual acclamation, which – as closely as I can reproduce it here – went thus:

'What do we think of Lord Cecil?' the president asked.

'First class!' responded the students.

'Who says so?'

'We do.'

'Who are we?'

'It's all of us!'

'Hip-hip!'

'Hurray!'

'Hip-hip!'

'Hurray!'

'Hip-hip!'

'Hurray!'

The girls are no less enthusiastic in their cheering than the males, but they are careful not to shout 'hurray' instead of 'hurrah', preferring the latter pronunciation as more formally correct.

13 October

The sense of and respect for hierarchy. Yesterday, before Lord Cecil's speech began, I was given a small lesson in this. When I arrived at the Union auditorium, there was still hardly anyone there. I enquired of one of the staff:

'Is this where Mr. Cecil is giving his lecture?'

Mr. Cecil! What insidiously mischievous demon induced me to change the honourable viscount's title, having never before referred to him as anything other than by his title of Lord. I simply could not believe it myself.

But even more surprised was the porter. He stretched himself up; short of stature as he was, he visibly gained height; and, lowering his gaze with great dignity, speaking in a tone of corrective censure, before answering my question, he said:

'Lord Cecil.'

14 October

In England people say not only 'my father and mother' but also 'my mother and father'.

19 October

Nowhere else have I seen women showing their legs like they do here. 'It's the Paris fashion,' everybody says. But the truth is that in Paris most women wear longer skirts. Young women here, in general, display their legs in a sporty way, as we might say; but beyond this the display often takes on other characteristics. And other proportions too. And as their legs are so long – and so well-turned, it must be said – it does seem that they are making more of an exhibition. It is certainly true that, upon embarking on any Channel ferry, crowded with English women, one has the sensation that, all of a sudden, skirts have become shorter.

21 October

I talked about religion with my students. I hold even more

firmly now to the impression that I formed last year: they have very little idea about what distinguishes the sects to which they belong.

29 October

Last night a terribly strong wind was blowing. One could hear the noise of slates being torn from roofs and falling to the ground. It seemed as if the windows were going to be blown in. Our beds shuddered. Now it is a calm, sunny morning. I regret not having kept count of how many days we have seen the sun since arriving here: in this respect, one's idea of English weather is exaggerated. I intend to keep a record as from today.

My notes – with each full stop indicating a separate day – form this little poem, as it might be called, covering the months of November–December 1927, in Oxton:

Rain. Rain. Sun in the afternoon. Sun in the morning.
Dead sun above the trees.
Sun. Sun. Sun. Sun in the morning.
Rain. Some sunshine. Outbreaks of rain.
Sun in the morning, just a little in the afternoon.
Sun mid-morning.
Thick cloud, rain.
Thick cloud, rain.
Thick cloud, rain: fine mist.
Low leaden sky: fog.
Fog.
Sun. Sun. Sun.
Exquisite sunshine. (I am writing by the open window,

basking in it.) Sunny periods.

Dark. *Dark.*

Thick cloud. Thick cloud.

A moment's sunshine. Some brief instants of sunshine.

THICK, DARK CLOUD. (Seven days of it.)

Sun. Snow. Sun. Sun.

Sunny in the morning. Snowfall.

Three days of whiteout (what has happened?).

Thick cloud. (Christmas.)

Sun. Five sunny days.

New Year's Eve.

1 November

Among people who practise walking as a sporting activity, there is a curious modality of this: it is engaged in by those who participate in night-time outings, people who under-take an 'all-night tour' and keep walking throughout a whole night.

3 November

At the Playhouse: *The Cradle Song* (*Canción de cuna*, by Martínez Sierra).[9] Not a very enthusiastic reception: on one side of me a young man was falling asleep – perhaps as a tribute to the piece's title. The general response contrasted somewhat with that which was later accorded to *Shall We Join the Ladies,* by Barrie.

9   Gregorio Martínez Sierra (Madrid, 1881–1947), popular Spanish poet and playwright.

5 November

Reading Freud was becoming so widespread among University people that the librarian has now removed that author's works from public access, making them available only upon application. A lecturer from the School of Engineering requested them.

'Are you interested in such topics?' the librarian asked him half in jest.

'No, I am not. They are for my wife.'

'Oh! In that case I can't help you,' the librarian pronounced, and he put the volume back on the shelf.

8 November

I had heard it said that in England the beliefs and practices of spiritualism were very widespread. Miss B had recounted to me a number of cases which had made an impression on her. I wanted to bring the subject up in conversations with my students: there was no way I could get them to talk about it. The students were no wiser about it than I was.

14 November

To go to her first dancing lesson, Miss B has taken a bath, curled her hair and put on a very special dress. Last year she confided in me that her ideal would be to become a 'dancing girl'.

24 November

Today dawned splendidly bright and clear. After the preceding three days of unending gloom, how to explain that fresh, vernal gentleness in the air? On such limpid days when I arrive back from Liverpool, getting off the tram close to our house, I am struck by the marked difference in the air quality between the two places: this feeling comes over me, softly insinuating itself, in such a way that I instinctively breathe deeply.

10 December

A Swiss maid has been forced to leave England because she did not notify the police that she had changed her place of residence. 'I don't want to go, because I have done nothing wrong,' she protested. Even so, go she must. And, as a special concession, she has been allowed a fortnight's grace.

12 December

The tram was packed, but there was still room for a girl who got on and squeezed in to sit beside me: she was slim, delicate, timid-looking, of the *sentimental* type.* We were so close together that her arm and her body were pressed against me. And from time to time I felt that arm of hers tremble. In fact she was all of a shiver, something which was well explained by the freezing morning and her insubstantial clothing. But, after a while, the human warmth which filled the vehicle must have revived her and she stopped shivering. And I became absorbed again in reading my newspaper.

When I looked up for a moment, I realised that the tram had started to empty and that I had room to edge away on the seat. I was about to do this when I saw that my neighbour also

* See entry for 19 January, 1928.

had space on her other side. I thought it would be impolite to make the first move. And so we stayed, pressed close together, until we were virtually the only two left on the long bench seat, almost alone in the vehicle, which was quickly becoming colder and colder. What must we have looked like, sitting there in such close contact, so still and so silent too? Would any observer have believed that we were two complete strangers, two distant lives with only that one point of contiguity, in silence, two bodies in something much more than incidental contact, very soon to be separated, each of us going into our own orbit, doubtless as distant one from the other as before?

And so it was. Even though heading in the same direction, our ways parted: I went below ground, to catch the Mersey Railway; she must have crossed the river on one of the ferries that ply back and forth, tucking herself away in a quiet corner while most of the other people on board, thickly and noisily herded together there, would be striding purposefully back and forth on the deck to keep themselves warm, and conspicuously putting into practice the slogan: 'For health and wealth travel by boat'.

13 December

Lowering sky. A sort of darkness I had not seen here previously, experienced only when visiting London. Smoke billowing white from chimneys into the dark fog. Birds clustering in the trees. Sparrows cheeping. By one o'clock in the afternoon it was as though night was drawing in. Here and there lights were coming on in windows. An hour later the day began to brighten up – with a strange sort of clarity which all around picked out and enhanced the whiteness of things (painted woodwork on houses, curtains).

14 December

At around 9 o'clock this morning it began to snow. Soon everything was white over. This broke the monotony: it was a different sort of monotony. 'We are not going to Switzerland,' I thought to myself, 'Switzerland is coming to us.' Then, in the afternoon, the fog, the dirty sky, the snow turned into dark slush. How far away the Alps seemed![10]

18 December

English houses look comfortable enough inside, but when cold weather really bites, this is not at all the case. The windows do not have shutters, nor, very often, thick curtains either. Fires are lit in a couple of rooms: everywhere else is freezing. It is an irrevocable principle never to use the fireplaces in bedrooms. The doctor has told Miss C. to light the fire in the room where she sleeps. But she prefers to be cold and suffer the effects of this on her health rather than to break the tradition. 'I don't want you to, absolutely don't want it,' she told Miss B. who was preparing a fire in the grate. And the girl had to obey.

19 December

The sky is so tenuously blue! A broad, pinkish white strip joins it with the earth. Clumps of trees on distant horizons fade into

10   Soldevila's wife Yvonne was Swiss, and Soldevila alludes here to what would presumably have been their usual family Christmas.

the haze. Occasional houses can be made out in between, with their multiple reddish chimneys as big as watch-towers. How appealing this landscape is to me!

25 December

Christmas. – Pearl-grey sky above the wet roofs shining like sealskin. Every now and then a snowflake, drifting and turning in the icy breeze. Bluish mist blurring the view of leafless woods. Everything enveloped in a religious silence ('A great silence is hovering over the whole of England,' I heard it announced.) And, suddenly, mid-morning, a joyous and crystal-sharp concert of bells.

From next door, through the wall, I have been able to hear for some time the chattering of young children. Their first glance, immediately upon waking up, will have been towards the head of their bed. Last night, as is the tradition, they hung a stocking there – one of their mother's, to enable more things to be fitted in – and, during the night Saint Nicholas/Santa Claus has filled it with attractive small presents: toys, sweets, fruit, other smaller stockings containing more playthings and treats.

The adults have also had their presents. Everybody, relatives and friends, exchange or send gifts. The value of these is often small, but it is touching to see how generalised is this exchange of gifts. Then everybody, old and young, gathers round the Christmas tree, hung with its decorations and its multicoloured candles, with cotton-wool snowflakes, and with English flags displaying the motto 'Saint George for Merry England!'

Flowers and holly sprigs provide some adornment to the dining room. There are too, here and there, bunches of mistletoe under which kisses are given and received, since in England the privilege of giving a kiss under the mistletoe is not an exclusively male one, as it is in other countries. Nor does it always come entirely for free: the custom has still not completely disappeared whereby the person, he or she, giving the kiss offers a present to the one kissed: a pair of gloves for the ladies, a tie for the men, this was the tradition in times gone by. There are still women who, recalling the good old days, will tell you that they received in a single Christmas half a dozen pairs of gloves.

Religious ceremonies take up a good part of the morning. Christmas communion is one of the most important for the Anglican religion. The rest of the morning in certain homes is occupied by preparation of the celebratory dinner – only at the highest social level is this formal repast taken in the evening. It centres around the turkey or goose, well stuffed and seasoned, and Christmas pudding. In fact, though, since the days of Dickens the goose has had to give way very largely to the turkey on the Christmas table.

On this day of the year, in England, no-one, not even the poorest, seems to go short of mouth-watering food. There are societies that organise special Christmas collections and use the proceeds to buy poultry for poor people. The markets are stocked high and wide with geese and turkeys. In Liverpool's St. John's Market row upon row of them reach half way up to its vast canopy. The crowd walks between walls of poultry, slaughtered, plucked and ready for cooking. People move along, unhurried and without pushing, and above all without loud shouting. Just listen. Conversations with stall-holders – male or female – take place in a normal tone, that is, with voices kept down. And stall-holders of either sex do not shout loudly to announce what they have for sale: they just speak in a slightly raised voice.

This is impressive. But there is something else which is even much more so. Look. In one place there is a gap in the great row of turkeys and geese. This space is filled by a row of something else: wreaths, crosses and bouquets of flowers to be taken to honour the dead during these days of solemnity and reflection.

One has a strange feeling at the sight, amid so much Pantagruelian abundance, of these flowers destined to wither or freeze on so many graves. The immediate reaction is that this is something grotesque and unsettling, but then it seems comforting, reassuring as to the warmth of people's feelings for one another. The effect is like that which one experiences on returning from a burial service performed in the fog or the wind of a harsh English winter, entering the house of the deceased and sitting close to the fire, around the table with the abundant fare on display. The contrast, for those not accustomed to experiencing it, is violently extreme: the first impression is of a kind of profanation. But, gradually, seeing everyone making an effort to appear composed, seeing the lady of the house greeting the mourners and even showing a slight smile despite her reddened eyes, hearing the conversations timidly beginning and slowly becoming normal, then you seem to understand that in this peculiar tribute to the deceased person, in this immediate renewal of life in one of its most essential aspects, there is something vitally instructive for those who are left behind, and a kind of assurance of everlastingness among them for the departed one. You feel that the person you have just previously left in that deep, damp hole in the ground will not be too separated from the everyday lives of those people who are now, around the table, associating the memory of them with this funeral repast.

Thus it is not strange that the days of Christmas, beyond the religious, family-centred and gastronomic significance they have in other countries, should in England have something of the character of what we associate with All Souls days. And, on reflection, this is fitting: because Christmas, the celebration of Christ's birth, does it not have the power to bring forcefully to the front of our minds the memory of departed loved ones?

The whole occasion places a veil of affection upon people's spirits, and you, as foreigners, through the simple fact of having spent Christmas among them, are given the feeling of having entered into a deeper intimacy with those around you.

26 December

How curious it is to see, here, well-built young men walking along by themselves, pushing their baby in its pram. Can one even imagine such a thing in our country?

8 January 1928

Marvellous day. The bricks and roof tiles of the houses, in the sunshine, were giving a kind of tender sigh. It must have been of such a day that Shelley wrote:

And makes the wintry world appear
As one on whom thou smilest, dear.

12 January

Courtesy on the tram. – I believe I am acquiring a big store of observations on how people behave on trams, especially on the politeness or rudeness they display when on board. And I enjoy making comparisons between different countries. This has sometimes helped me to see things in perspective. Thus, for example, in Barcelona, a dozen or so years ago, in order to combat the inconsiderateness of men who did not give up their seats for female passengers, it was put about that such behaviour did not happen in Madrid. However, at the time, the way of things in Madrid was exactly the same as in Barcelona, which is to say that there were some men who, politely, gave up their seats for ladies while others stayed put.

It used also to be remarked that, on this same subject, that men abroad, on trams and other forms of public transport, did not offer their seat to a lady. One still hears this said, and it is often repeated. 'Advances in civilisation,' one person will say; 'Sport is to blame,' says somebody else; 'Don't they want equality with men?' a third person asks, mischievously. 'It's the same abroad.'

But this is not strictly true, and, as regards England, it is quite false. I think that my experience as a tram user is sufficient to enable me to reach conclusions. During the whole of the last academic year and thus far into the present one, to get to the University I have had to use combinations of at least three different modes of transport: train-ferry-tram; train-underground (or, more accurately, sub-marine)-tram; tram-underground-tram. So, after all the observations I have had the opportunity to make, my conclusion is as follows: it is unusual here to see any man staying in his seat whenever there is a lady standing.

And yet, this is the country of sport, the country of the suffragettes, the country of camaraderie between the two sexes.

Obviously there are some exceptions, but they really are exceptional, especially among the upper and the middle classes. And, also, if you see a man who does not give up his seat, you must wonder whether he does not have some disability that explains his behaviour; when he gets up, you will perhaps see that he is lame, and the woman standing right in front of him probably relinquished her seat to him as soon as he limped unsteadily onto the tram.

So what we have observed in general is not exactly a simple gesture of politeness paid by men to women: it is an act of consideration shown by the stronger person towards the weaker one. This is why a youngster or a girl will quickly get to their feet if there is not a seat for a lady or for an elderly person who needs one. 'I'm growing old,' the character in a play remarks, 'I'm getting old: as soon as I get on a tram young women immediately give up their seats for me.'

This is a good thing, a most stimulating example which one would like to see implanted back home. Here, in many cases, is behaviour which carries a sharp lesson. What would be the reaction of a healthy young man who did not give up his seat to an elderly lady and who then saw a young woman hastening to do what he should have done? Rather than complaining about men's lack of good manners, what women ought to do is to show them which way courtesy lies: to make them react by embarrassing them through example.

And, last but not least, women themselves should show

that they appreciate the small act of courtesy shown to them. It has been remarked that sometimes, in our country, you can give up your seat for a lady and she does not even thank you. Others do acknowledge the gesture with a curt, barely perceptible muttered word or two. Then, finally, there are yet others who respond with a show of bad temper or – who knows? – of concealed shyness. It is unusual for the woman involved – whether old or young, middle class or working class – to look at you in a friendly way and to thank you clearly and distinctly. In England it is usually the other way round, and 'thank you', 'thanks very much' generally spring forth clear and expressive, even in the exceptional case of your offer being refused.

The most curious thing, however, is that the English themselves consider such good-mannered behaviour to be a custom now in decline, no longer on the increase as it was some years ago. Back then, evidently, the few exceptions to the rule encountered nowadays simply did not occur.

Even so, most Englishmen (I think I dare generalise from observations made in Lancashire and Cheshire) continue to behave in this matter like true gentlemen, and it is to them that we should look when we invoke the foreign model for correctness in the delicate issue of courtesy on the tram.

17 January

Poets' Country. – Remembering our poets is not something that is much cultivated among us. I do not refer to memory of their works as much as to the memory that we might call biographical: an interest which arises not from indiscreet curiosity but one which leads naturally from knowledge of their works to knowledge about their lives, something which gives to the latter dimension a devotional status, creating around the figure of the individual poet an atmosphere very similar to that of religious devotion.

I have great admiration for 19th century English poetry, and this makes me wish that there was an anthology, prepared by the best poets in the Catalan language, of its major representatives. But I do have the impression that the exalted prestige enjoyed by that body of poetry is due not only to its true literary excellence, but also to the devotion which the English public created around their poets. And what is true of the English applies also to the Scots.

In both England and Scotland there are regions which are referred to by the name of some great poet who was born or who lived there, rather than by the place's official name: Stratford and its surrounding area are regularly known as 'Shakespeare Country'; the English Lake District has also been designated 'Wordsworthshire', for obvious reasons; Ayrshire, in South-West Scotland, is often called 'Burns Country'; the region centred on Melrose is covered by the generic name 'Scott's Land', in memory of Sir Walter, who lived for twenty years in Abbotsford.

I do not know whether anything similar has arisen in other countries, and certainly no such cases have come to my attention. What I do know is that, in general, any district which can pride itself in having been the birthplace of a great poet, or in having been where a part of the poet's life was spent, will always remember the fact with satisfaction and even pride. But this, also in general, has no more than accidental importance for the place in question, perhaps the most important of all the 'accidents' in its history, but in the end nothing more than that.

On the other hand, in England and in Scotland, in the cases already referred to, a region has been put in a position of dependency upon a poet, so much so for the impression to be given that it is not the place which conditioned the poet's life, but rather that the latter had a formative effect on the life of the former. While in all these places there are venerable monuments, wonderful landscapes, memories of heroic deeds, all of this seems to have been put at the service of the poet, in order to accentuate or to frame his memory. In the Scottish Borders, for example, there are the ruins of Melrose Abbey, founded in the twelfth century by the King of Scotland David I, reconstructed in the fourteenth century by Robert the Bruce, the hero of Scottish independence. They are considered to be the most impressive ruins in all Scotland: Bruce's heart was interred there. Nevertheless, the main claim to fame is that Sir Walter Scott resided hereabouts, while the melancholy beauty of the abbey and all the history preserved there have become details which set in greater relief that prominent biographical feature.

Phenomena such as this do not come about without a special mind-set of a people regarding their poets, however great might be the literary stature of the writers in question. If anyone were to ask us to tell them about the countryside around Vic, would we think to tell them that, first and foremost, this is the region where the great writer Jacint Verdaguer[11] spent

11   Born in 1845, in the small village of Folgueroles (close to the regional capital of Vic), Verdaguer was a charismatic priest whose troubled life made him very popular, even something of a cult figure, in Catalonia towards the end of the nineteenth century. He produced some fine lyrical poetry as well as the two ambitious epic compositions (*L'Atlàntida* [1877] and *Canigó* [1886]) which established his status as Catalonia's 'national poet', in a period when the modern Catalan revival movement, in culture and in politics, was gathering significant momentum.

much of his life? Probably not. On the other hand, if you ask an Englishman about Stratford-upon-Avon, he will be very quick to recall that this was where Shakespeare was born. And if you bring the Lake District into the conversation it is certain that, as well as singing the praises of its marvellous countryside, he will not neglect to remind you of the 'Lake School of Poetry' which flourished there.

This intimate association of a place and an author suggests also, undoubtedly, that the writer had a special involvement in those particular geographical surroundings. It implies, first of all, that he spent long periods of residence there. It implies a special kind of local popularity. It implies, in sum, a close relationship between the writing and the landscape. In Sussex, near to Horsham, lies Field Place, where Shelley was born and where he spent his childhood. But because he never afterwards resided there for any significant length of time, because his work on the whole is not directly linked to his birthplace and is not thus susceptible to the kind of popularity which has come to surround the work of Wordsworth, of Burns or of Scott, there is no such place nowadays as 'Shelley Country'.

On the other hand, I would not be surprised if, a few years from now, there were not in England a 'Hardy Country' commemorating the great novelist and poet who died recently.*12

*   My prediction was accurate: so accurate, that many years before his death [1928] Hardy's Wessex already existed, the object of a cult comparable to that of Scott. I was informed of this by Professor E. Allison Peers of Liverpool University, shortly before these jottings went to press, who told me that thirty years ago he had published a book on the subject. Ten years after that he spent a three-week holiday visiting the places mentioned in the novels. I am indebted to Professor Peers for this and other similarly helpful observations, a debt which I am pleased to acknowledge here.

12   I have been unable to find any evidence of the existence of the book mentioned in the note above. One suspects a lapse of memory on Soldevila's part, or perhaps that the famously self-important Peers might have tried to impress his junior colleague, on the basis of a three-week holiday in Wessex.

19 January

There are two sorts of typically English girls: what we could call the *sporty* type and what we could call the *sentimental* one. The first is characteristically tall, strong, very well built, with a long and purposeful stride, head held high, a healthy skin tone and, above all, a steely gaze which is both intensely proud and somewhat challenging. The other is the short, slim type, rather flat-breasted, with a gentle look in her pale-blue eyes, walking along with hands clasped in front of her holding a purse below her waist-line. These two radically opposed types seem to me to symbolise two absolutely fundamental aspects of English life: the 'hearth and home' and the sports field.

21 January

Immense park in Birkenhead. It was a great delight to see, everywhere you looked, close by or away in the distance, through a curtain of heavy rain, the swarming movements of rugby matches in progress.

28 January

I went to the Argyle theatre. I went because I was told that it is the theatre of 'low Birkenhead'. The show was a revue called *Mixed Bath*. What a theatre, what a revue and what an audience! On stage, scrawny flesh, gaunt bodies, such as to inspire pity. Among the audience, haggard faces, degenerate looks. But, even so, not poverty-stricken people. Rather, people who do not have much to eat. The ticket prices are hardly cheap (three shillings for a seat in the orchestra stalls). But, despite this, the public have low expectations. It is inconceivable that a French or a Catalan audience would put up with an exhibition of women like that without noisy protest. These spectators put up with it, not out of pity, but because their taste is not more demanding. They get sentimental at the mawkish songs, and they laugh uproariously at the crudely grotesque tableaux; I think that they must even be dazzled by what they see as the beauty of the female artistes. In short: they go there with an innocent determination to enjoy themselves. They even applaud the orchestra conductor (some orchestra! and such songs!) and he bows ceremoniously, dressed in a dinner jacket just like all his musicians.

3 February

Attracting foreign tourists. – Seeing the abundance of posters used, in other countries, for tourist publicity, I have wondered more than once why this powerful medium of suggestion and stimulation is so greatly neglected back home in Catalonia. I should like to know whether, when travelling abroad, you have ever seen in railway stations, alongside posters inviting you to journey to diverse distant countries, from Egypt to Norway, any advertisement proclaiming the delights of your own land and its coast. I cannot recall having seen any, and I would almost dare to say that none exists. And in Catalonia itself, are there many to be seen? Here and now, rack my brain as I may, I cannot bring to mind a single one, although some vague recollection of an advertisement for Montserrat[13] does

13   An important Benedictine monastery in the hills north-west of Barcelona, Montserrat, which dates from the 11th century, has had a significant role in the religious life and the community history of Catalonia, from the earliest times to the present. The monastery and

seem to be working its way to the surface. Whether this corresponds or not to something actually seen, the fact is that tourist publicity through the medium of the poster can be considered non-existent in our country.*

It is a pity. The impact of this kind of advertising must be very effective for it to be on display on such a grand scale in countries which make quite a living from tourism, like Switzerland, or which provide a sizeable contingent of tourists, like England. The medium's power of suggestion and ability to stimulate interest are beyond dispute. When viewing this array of posters, varying in artistic merit, but often done with eye-catching deftness, who will not feel stirring within them the urge to get to know the places advertised? It might be this blue lake, bounded by lofty snow-clad mountains, with a sturdy medieval castle on its shore; or another where the snow has disappeared to leave behind the gentle greenness of meadowland and a sky smiling charmingly between sweet-natured clouds; that town with its dark ancient houses, caressed by the constant presence of still water and the reflections therein; or that other town, tucked up close to a towering castle which can be made out through a bluish haze; and this country where there seems to be only flat fields and a vast sky; and this promontory topped by a gothic abbey with sea on all sides; and this golden beach; and these silvery waterfalls, so immense; and this tiny village of wooden houses, glowing red in the

its associated buildings occupy a commanding site high up among the jagged pinnacles of the Montserrat massif. It is still a special place of worship and pilgrimage, centred on the figure of *La Moreneta*/the Black Virgin, the Mother of God of Montserrat, while being also nowadays a big attraction for secular tourism from far and near. Soldevila is writing just before the first wave of popular tourist interest in Spain was to gather momentum in the 1930s, as is evidenced in his own footnote immediately below.

*   Subsequently the whole situation has changed considerably.

sunset, and so very many other corners of the world that are set before us here, captured in their most attractive poses. Here we have an invitation to travel, no less compelling than that expressed to Musset by the Muse:

> *Partons, nous sommes seuls, l'univers est à nous:*
> *Voici la verte Écosse et la brune Italie.*
> *Et la Grèce, ma mere, où le miel est si doux.*[14]

And these publicity posters are found not only in railway stations, travel agencies or hotels, but in other places too: a few days ago in a Liverpool department store I was surprised to come across a whole collection, for various spots in the Swiss Alps. And such posters constitute just one part of the graphic advertising material, which is complemented by large displays in the press, photographs in railway compartments, free brochures. What can be more tempting for a well-to-do Englishman (of which there is no shortage) than these adverts for the French Riviera which appear in the major English newspapers, inviting him to leave behind the chilly British mists and to enjoy the sun and the warmth of the Côte d'Azure. The comfort of the travel, the favourable rate of exchange, the delightful places in which to stay, everything is put across in perfectly convincing terms, especially for those who feel the compunction, as do many English people, not to stay for too long in one place, and who are blessed with such a buoyant currency and such an inhospitable climate.

The same could be said about the brochures. These often combine splendid photography with well-written texts which

14   'Let us away, for we are alone and the world is ours;/ here is green Scotland and bronzed Italy,/and Greece, my mother, where the honey is so sweet.'

are sometimes the work of a writer of some standing. Right now I have before me a prospectus for Engelberg – 'Prize bloom of the Alps' – written by the novelist Le Queux.

All of this could be brought about in our country. I will not say that nothing is done in this direction, but what there is falls short, is meagre and passes almost unnoticed. Nevertheless, we have everything required. Ours is a country where we can go from blue coastlines to Alpine glaciers, we have excellent landscape artists, we have first-rate writers. In these three elements travel agencies, transport companies, tourist promotion bodies, hoteliers of all grades and restaurateurs possess an infinite treasure to benefit from. What would certainly have to be ensured at the same time, though, is that the delights of all there is to be seen should not be blurred by a thousand inconveniences and irritations, and that short journeys in Catalonia should not prove more expensive – as they often do now – than long journeys made abroad.

5 February

The horizon: I am it. Beyond these roof-tops is the horizon, right there, close enough to touch. And beyond that, nothing. Or rather, infinity.

11 February

I have been to see *Potiphar's Wife*.[15] The most controversial work of recent times, according to the publicity. They have

---

15   The author, Edgar C. Middleton (1894–1939) went on to enjoy some success as a cinema screenwriter in the 1930s. Lawrence Olivier was in the cast of the film version of *Potiphar's Wife* (1931).

theatre censorship in England. 'What was the censor doing?' I asked. 'He was asleep', was the answer.

There is an entire act completely taken up by a Lady so-and-so's preparations to seduce her chauffeur – *déshabillé*, perfume, subtle lighting – followed by the whole seduction scene in sleeveless, low-cut night-dress, with her in suggestive poses, reclining on the divan, etc. All the rest of the play revolves around this. The chauffeur, who has put up resistance, is accused by the lady and sent to prison. Lord so-and-so behaves despicably. His lady wife and a friend of hers lie through their teeth. The chauffeur's defending counsel manages to demonstrate his innocence.

The seduction scene is carried off very elegantly, it must be said. Imbuing her performance with a convincing erotic charge, the actress also deploys considerable delicacy and a certain child-like playfulness which amusingly lighten the action. The public follow the performance very attentively. But, at the end of the act, despite the actress's fine interpretation of her part, there was no applause at all.

12 February

I am reliably informed that in England being adulterous can still create many difficulties for a man's prospects in his career: in banking, big business, etc. I have heard of the case of an Englishman who fought in the occupation of Cologne at the end of the Great War and who, having had a mistress in that city, had not been allowed to return afterwards to the merchant bank where he used to work.

14 February

St. Valentine's Day. – This is the day when young men send written declarations of love to the girls. But if it is a leap year then it is the girls who write to the boys. Except among the lower classes, the tradition is dying out.

16 February

Around mid-day several coach-loads of students from Manchester arrived at the University. They came to sell their Rag magazine, raising funds for local hospitals. This coincided with the rowdy election here of 'Sister Jane', the University mascot, and with the rivalry between Faculties to take possession of her. Strictly she should go to the Faculty which has collected the most money on 'Panto Day'. But eventually it turns into a physical struggle to carry off the prize. The students who stood aloft on one of the floats, to declare the results of the fund-raising, remained undaunted as they were subjected to a sustained bombardment of flour-bombs and bad fruit. The chemists created a great cloud of smoke which enveloped the quadrangle and caused a temporary evacuation. The girls did not get involved in the horse-play, staying on the edges of the all-male mêlée and scurrying at the slightest disturbance towards the exits. The engineers won the day. The winners are the Faculty or the School which has 'Sister Jane' in their possession at five o'clock in the afternoon. The 'Sister' they fight over is a processional figure constructed on a wooden frame.

22 February

The days seem so long! Twilight lasts for ever.

24 February

I went to a Jewish theatre show. Out and about one sees a lot of them, obviously; but it was curious to see so many gathered together in that large hall and to hear their strange English with Hebrew mixed in. Dark skins, narrow faces with sharp noses, or plump faces with flattened noses, bovine eyes, heavily made-up women, very noisy laughter, quick movements, very pushy attitudes (while the show was going on, a lot of them sat leaning forwards to rest their arms on the row of seats in front); the entire audience made up of Jews. The programmes, printed in the Hebrew alphabet. The play itself, performed in their hybrid language.

28 February

Mock elections. – English young people are trained very early for the struggles they will have to endure later in life. Just as small children imitate in their play those things that most impress them in the lives of grown-ups (soldiers or hunters, farmers or sailors, mothers or nannies), so adolescents and youths play at what they would like to do seriously within a very short time when, having reached adulthood, they will become involved in life's free-for-all. And those earlier games are thus a most useful preparation. So it is with the mock political elections which have just been held in the University, imitating in all respects proper parliamentary elections. Oral and printed propaganda, vigorous debates, rallies, voting, formal declaration of results, formation of a government, even a speech from the throne: nothing at all has been omitted.

A few days beforehand, posters for the elections organised by the Guild of Undergraduates or Students' Union appeared in the University corridors, on the special boards for student announcements (where dances, tea-parties, debates, special lectures etc are advertised) and elsewhere on the premises. I have kept some of these posters, given to me by students. Three candidates are officially standing: one Conservative ('gentleman'), a Labourite (mill-girl) and a Liberal (solicitor). Also announced are rallies, on February 20, 21 and 23, with the polls to be held, using individual voting slips, on the 22nd and 23rd, closing at 2pm.

For the past few days there has been a noticeable effervescence among the students. My own pupils have kept me up to date on the vicissitudes of the electoral campaign. One of them was flushed with excitement at his intervention in the hustings: he had created hilarious laughter among those present by denouncing Russian infiltration in the Labour Party, presenting documentary evidence (a caricature of that which the actual government has been claiming to have found), and unmasking the fair-haired mill-girl who is denounced as a Slav, no Englishwoman she. The humour of all this was the more sharply marked by the fact that this particular young man was known to have Labour sympathies and to be of Jewish descent.

Next day, however, I went to a Liberal gathering, and while I was expecting to find a flood of humour, what I encountered was impressive seriousness. A youth was speaking with great aplomb; male and female students were listening to him in silence, the latter displaying an impressive row of strong legs and rounded knees. (In my notebook I find this jotting: 'row girls legs: the race is in no danger in this respect.')

The elections took place without any kind of incident, giving the following result: Liberal 245 votes; Conservatives, 145; Labour, 140.

The Labour vote, almost equalling the Conservative one, in an institution where there is not a single member of the working class, is extremely significant: it signifies that a sector of the intelligentsia and of people professing liberal views would vote Labour, alongside the proletariat, in the next election when it is held. The Liberal triumph seems to announce a high degree of idealistic expectation, predicting a substantial majority for Lloyd George's followers. The Conservative vote expresses tiredness in the country regarding the party's policies and performance in government. This is to be explained, for sure, by the fact that the voters were young people, among whom there were actually few representatives of the highest tiers of English society (the scions of the wealthiest classes usually going to Oxford and Cambridge to study).

Respecting the wish of the people, the Liberals straight away formed a government. In line with the declared preference of the female electorate, half of the posts in the administration went to women. During a 'Parliamentary Evening', the new government was introduced to the House (the student body). The session was presided over by a real-life Liberal MP, because such mock events and play-acting are often gladly supported by people who are already on the career ladder. But neither the presence of this personage nor the solemnity of the King's speech sufficed to prevent the rather un-parliamentary racket or the hail of paper darts aimed at the government.

2 March

A speech by Lloyd George. – Saint David, after whom Lloyd George is named, is also the patron saint of Wales. Every year, on the first day of March, the Welsh celebrate in the Saint's honour various festivities: religious, musical and gastronomic. At one such event, the annual patriotic dinner of the Cardiff Cymrodorian Society, Lloyd George himself took part, giving a speech which was broadcast on the radio and which, by this means, I was able to listen to. Before he began I heard all the acclamations, applause and cheering to which the diners were moved by the resonant announcement that they were about to be addressed by the Honourable David Lloyd George. I heard also the tuneful rendition of *For He's a Jolly Good Fellow* which is usually sung by all present at such occasions.

Lloyd George speaks slowly, something that I find rather unusual in this country. Perhaps nowhere else, apart from in the Madrid Ateneo,[16] have I heard orators speak as fast as they do here in England. My impression, however, is that the better the speaker, the more measured is the delivery. The phenomenon is perhaps not exclusive to this country, but there is no doubt that it is nevertheless a very curious one. The most quick-fire oratory I ever heard in England came from a soap-box speaker in Trafalgar Square; and it is not surprising that the most unhurried delivery I have encountered was in

16   Private club (founded in 1835) with the object of promoting cultural, intellectual and artistic activities. The social aspect of the institution inevitably fostered political debate.

a speech by the Prince of Wales, who places noble pauses between each and every word.

But Lloyd George not only speaks with great deliberation, he is also most attentive to nuances of emphasis, something which I find to be even more exceptional than slowness in speech-making as practised here. A noticeably unvaried tone, perhaps a certain sameness in expression, seem to me to be characteristics of present-day English oratory. Someone who has begun speaking energetically and in an accentuated manner does not throttle back or drop into a more restrained voice, or vice-versa. Lloyd George, however, whose speaking manner is generally high-pitched, does not refrain from moving now and then into the deeper ranges. Without overdoing it, of course, and always at a respectful distance in this regard from some of his Spanish counterparts. His sharp notes are not exactly the same, but they do evoke for me the oratorical manner of the Pere Coromines[17] that I heard as an adolescent. As regards the Welsh politician's way of engaging and winning over his listeners, judging by the speech of his I am referring to, we must conclude that, like many public speakers in England, he prefers to deploy humour rather than pathos, and that he seeks laughter rather than applause from those he is addressing.

He opened his speech with a few words in Welsh. The r's rolled and the gutturals grated; but straight away, after an outburst of laughter from the audience, he switched to English. Subsequently, from reports in the press, I got to the bottom of this. 'I should love,' he had said, 'to speak in the language of Saint David, but I think I shall do a greater service to Wales

17   (Barcelona 1870–Buenos Aires 1939): Catalan writer and politician.

if I speak in the language of the Gentiles.' Naturally, by being broadcast on the radio his speech was going out not just to Wales but to the whole of the United Kingdom. Last night all programmes carried at 9.30pm Lloyd George's speech.

It was a defence of small nations, beginning with his own: Wales. 'We are inspired,' he said, 'by a communal love for that beautiful little country and for its traditions. We are loyal to the throne, we are loyal to Great Britain, we are loyal to the Empire. But this does not exclude an intense loyalty to Wales.'

'There are those,' he added, 'who constantly attack the small nations. They write always as though there were too many of them. They are like the kind of people who every now and then write to the newspapers to complain that there are too many dogs, insisting that all dogs ought to be put down, except theirs. I admire the great wolf-hound, but have an intense affection for that intelligent, brave little creature known as the Welsh terrier. Since the Great War six new nations have come into being in Europe, and there are people who say that they are a big nuisance. There are too many of them. They interfere in affairs. They make life difficult for those who travel on diplomatic and commercial business. Nothing but commerce and traffic. Those who say such things are the superior peoples, and all superior peoples lack imagination. They would like to flatten the Alps, because they get in the way of commercial exchange between northern and southern Europe. They are the ones who talk always about economic objectives, economic entities, economic facts, and they forget that the first lesson, and the greatest lesson, in political economy is that man does not live by bread alone. The new small nations of Europe might be an inconvenience, but these countries have been given new life by the motive force of patriotism. It has unleashed new energies, raised the morale of the people, enlivened their intellectual life, aroused dormant impulses, and this will eventually bring about higher material standards of living. The supreme test that a nation is fit to live a life of its own is this: that it has managed, over the centuries, to survive oppression, tyranny and the disruptive forces which conspire to destroy national community. This test has been undergone by Wales over the centuries, and no other nation has passed it more convincingly.'

There is no need to say how fervently this passage of Lloyd George's speech was applauded. I identified myself with that applause, regretting only that the same piece of apparatus which relayed to me his sonorous words could not transmit back to him the loud expression of my agreement.

3 March

I went to the University sports ground. Endless, monotonous Liverpool: everywhere looks the same. Mist and fog, like a fine dust which seems to be rising up, just beyond where you are, further along the street you are in: you never quite get to where it is: you are never quite in fog, just for ever going into it. As you come to the outskirts of town, some wide, tree-lined avenues begin to be seen, with their typical red-brick and front gardens. In spring these thoroughfares must look very pretty.

A cemetery right inside the city, with no walls to hide it from view: streets running close alongside it, houses overlooking it, as though it were an urban square. Green turf and the greyish white of graves in long rows. Monumental masons have their workshops right next to the graveyard. Further out, the city seems to open up, to breathe. The fog becomes less dense. The houses look clean and well-tended. The city thins out and stretches of countryside are glimpsed. The tram moves along smoothly across grass on either side. After so much mud and so much ugliness, one's eyes are soothed by the greenness over which the vehicle is travelling.

University playing fields. Admission, sixpence. Two games of rugby are in progress, one soccer match, three of hockey and one of netball (the latter and one of the hockey games being played by female teams). The student spectators are of both sexes. There is no seating: because of the muddy surface you have to stand, on wooden slats laid out on the ground along the length of the pitches. What I found most interesting was the women's hockey. The swift attacking moves of the forwards are very pleasing to watch. Some of the players are very shapely and attractive (short hair, blue kit, a darker vest over a light-blue dress, hem-line well above the knee, black socks). But then there are others who look just like men.

No kind of shouting from the spectators. Just every now and then one hears, spoken rather than shouted out, words of encouragement for the home football team: 'Come on, Liverpool'. A fair-haired young fellow, one of the Liverpool players, heads the ball, and his hair-piece falls off. Girls looking away, pretending they have not noticed, blushing, spluttering with laughter.

The afternoon is fading. The outlines of trees in the distance become fainter. The houses look like ghosts of themselves. On the way back I meet groups of women students, walking, bare-headed, taking long strides, glowing. The city closes in. Suddenly, a big open space: the cemetery. The vast expanse of grass, in the mist, calls to mind the sports ground. Sport!

Cambridge, 9 March

It appears that for some time now, in competitive sports, Cambridge is ahead of Oxford. When their ancient buildings are compared, Oxford beats Cambridge. This is also so true as regards the respective urban landscapes. As for grounds and gardens, we shall still incline, but not without some hesitation, to see Oxford in the lead. Finally, if we are looking at the illustrious names that have come forth from one or other of these rival universities, we shall not know which one to favour and shall probably end up declaring it a draw. Because who could call the odds between Oxonian Duns Scotius, Locke, Thomas Hobbes, Jeremy Bentham, Adam Smith, Pitt the Elder, Wellington, Gladstone, Cardinal Newman, Addison, Ruskin, Matthew Arnold and Swinburne, on the one hand, and Newton, Bacon, Edmund Spenser, Marlowe, Robert and Horace Walpole, William Pitt the Younger, Thomas Gresham, Dryden, Macauley, Byron, Thackeray, Tennyson and Wordsworth, all Cambridge educated, on the other?

When their historic buildings are compared, as I say, Oxford beats Cambridge. It is more of an ancient city: it has more old colleges and these are less merged into the modern urban fabric. This is the difference between the two cities that you notice immediately: the difference arising from the number and the distribution of the colleges. Magnificent buildings like King's College in Cambridge suffer some small diminution in the prestige of their facades through the fact that they face directly not onto ancient and noble edifices, but rather

onto undistinguished modern houses and an array of ordi-
nary-looking shops. It would be hard to find in Cambridge
ensembles like that which in Oxford spreads out around the
Radcliffe Camera, or thoroughfares like Turl Street with Jesus
and Exeter Colleges, or like the junction of Grove Street and
Merton Street, or like New College Lane, parts and corners of
town where everything is, or seems, ancient – even the silence.

Perhaps only St. John's College and Queen's College in
Cambridge are in this regard comparable with what we have
in Oxford. In every other aspect, however, the individual
colleges in both cities are completely alike, and they could
be transplanted either way without any general detriment, so
fully of a kind are they. The similarities are striking: the styles
of building, the very colour of the stonework, the layout based
on quadrangles connected by narrow passages, the lawns which
carpet the courts, the garden-backed perspectives, the dining
halls adorned with portraits of illustrious personages who have
stayed in or graduated from the particular college, their long
tables for fellows and undergraduates (high table set on a low
dais, with chairs, while the students' tables are arranged at right
angles to it, with just benches); and finally, the same rather
cloying odour, a blend of cooking fats and cleanliness, issuing
from the kitchens and invading the adjoining quarters and
even those some distance away. To complete the symmetry,
even many of the names are the same: Corpus Christi College,
Divinity School, Magdalen College, Queen's College, St. John's
College, Pembroke College.

Certain Cambridge colleges – St. John's, for example – do
offer a noticeable difference from the Oxford ones and the
others in Cambridge itself: the buildings are mainly of brick

rather than stone. This is not to say, however, that the material is at odds with the beauty of the ancient architecture. Here we have a perhaps more restrained, a more modest beauty, but one which is no less fine. The old red bricks acquire a warm, matt presence. This is what makes St. John's one of the most attractive and most impressive of the Cambridge colleges. It has, moreover, a covered bridge over the River Cam, with iron grilles in the Gothic window spaces, which forms a uniquely picturesque corner of Cambridge. The water glides by slowly, very slow, beneath the bridge: water of a thick, opaque green where the grass of the meadows along its banks and the leaves of the willows that lightly touch the current seem to be dissolved. The bridge joins the old part of St. John's with the new part, one of those happy pieces of mock-Gothic which are found perhaps only in England. The river slips between the walls of the two sets of buildings, flowing under the Old Bridge a little further downstream and then out into gardens and grassland, the famous Backs of the colleges which are one of the wonders of Cambridge.

There is another thing that to my mind marks a distinction between the colleges of the two great English universities, and it is that in those of Cambridge it is most unusual to find that stark severity which is met in some of the Oxford ones. And altogether you feel that the weight of tradition is not so strong in Cambridge. Although it is the presence of the University which provides its glory, the new part of town seems to predominate, much vaster and intruding boldly on the old-world character of the ancient streets. You feel this less in Oxford, and it is one reason why the impression made upon the traveller is deeper there.

It must be admitted, though, that one's view of these two cities will depend to a great extent on the order in which they are visited. Surprise plays a large part in the admiration they arouse. We went without preconceived ideas, so that the one which we chose to go to first will have in its favour the charm of novelty. If, instead of starting with the Oxford colleges, I had visited first the Cambridge ones, I would have said basically as I have done just now: 'Yes: more of the same.'

And it is the same: one of the finest things to be found anywhere in the world. A creation into which monarchs and princes, prelates and noblemen have poured their munificence, aware of what it was they were building. And, in Cambridge, King's College Chapel, on account of its great size and its beauty, on account of its regal foundation, seems to symbolise that moral and material endeavour. Wordsworth, a pupil of St. John's, sang in an admirable sonnet of 'this immense and glorious work of fine intelligence', those lofty pillars, that fan-vaulted roof, the ten-thousand recesses where light and shade repose, where music dwells, lingering, and wandering on as though loath to die. And Wordsworth's sonnet is another title of nobility for the Chapel, considered to be the glory of King's College and the jewel in Cambridge's crown.

14 March

Chester. – I had passed through Chester several times before. The fame of the place, due to the double prestige of its old buildings and of its picturesque setting, had induced me to look eagerly, on every occasion, through the train window. Yet nothing had ever confirmed for me, nor even insinuated, any justification for that prestige. Endless roofs of sad slate, with their clusters of chimney pots forming crenellations set upon square, solid chimney stacks, just like you see in so many other English cities: that is all I had previously been able to make of the place. Of its magnificent cathedral, its ancient walls, its gated thoroughfares, its agreeable suburbs, of none of these had I been aware.* Nevertheless, these treasures were there for the asking: it was enough to open any guidebook to have their existence proclaimed. There could be no doubt: here was England's most thoroughly typical medieval city. As for its setting, I had sufficiently savoured the sweetness of the Cheshire landscape so as not to harbour any doubts about the placidity of the banks of the Dee thereabouts. So I promised myself a visit to Chester soon.

At last I was able to make the trip: at last, after the usual series of postponements that often keep us away from the things closest at hand, delaying our acquaintance with them – a reasonable explanation or excuse for those who are better acquainted with foreign parts than with their own country. At last I made the journey to Chester, and I was not disappointed. The cathedral is one of the noblest and finest I have ever seen; the encircling walls, although by no means comparable to those of Carcassonne, have stretches which are intensely steeped in history; the old arcades along many streets are superior to anything of the kind I have encountered elsewhere, from Berne to Ciutadella; the River Dee, running round one half of the city, half encloses it with meadows and vast, leafy woodland. And these are not the only delights of Chester.

* In fact, on subsequent occasions when I travelled through the city without stopping, I had to acknowledge that previously I had not been looking carefully enough.

On leaving the station and going towards the centre along City Road, I immediately had the sensation of being in a city quite different from Birkenhead or Liverpool, although these are nearby. The overall aspect, as seen from a distance on a moving train, might have been similar: but the houses beneath those roofs and the streets between the houses have a character all their own: much cleaner streets and houses that are much less dark and grim, while here and there, anticipating the wealth of traditional architecture I was expecting to encounter, there is the occasional half-timbered building, white walls with exposed timbers painted black. Soon, as one goes into Foregate Street, there are more and more examples of this traditional style. A gateway in the city wall divides the street or, rather, marks the beginning of another, and then, once through the gate, the arcades begin. Some of these are at street level, like those in medieval cities elsewhere, but others are constructed in a unique way which is typical of Chester: they run along what would be our mezzanine level, forming as it were long galleries above the shops and larger stores at street level. Access from the street is by small stairways, each with a wooden or iron banister, and a kind of ramp leading up to the steps. As at street level, there are also rows of shops in these arcades. This layout means that each building has twice the number of shops that it would otherwise house. Some of these are of very high quality and expensive, and the total impression is one of modernity and antiquity combined, not tastelessly but in a pleasingly harmonious way. This, together with the people who throng these streets – the nerve-centre of the city – completely immunises Chester against any impression of its being a dead city. It is not an ancient monument frozen in a past of centuries ago: its antiquity is vigorous and active, like that of certain old men who, despite their age and venerable aspect, communicate a much greater sense of vitality than many in their prime.

This is not to say that there are no parts of the city, quiet hidden corners, where the march of the centuries seems to have been halted. Abbey Square, flanking the cathedral, cut off from the urban clatter and din by a darkly imposing fourteenth century gateway, with no other noise than the chirping of sparrows, and with a plant-choked pond in the middle, is one of the most agreeable of these. And there are others too, along the inside of the walls, where the historical atmosphere seems still to hover. Here there is a tower from which Charles Stuart watched the fatal defeat of his troops at Rowton Moor, in 1645. Over there, in the distance, the ruins of Bleston Castle can still be made out; but nowadays the modern Chester extends from the city wall outwards, and it is in the other direction, into the area enclosed by the wall, towards the magnificent cathedral, that one's eyes are drawn.

Coming through East Gate, you are suddenly surprised by the sight of it. It rises up, like so many other English churches, close to the edge of a grass-covered cemetery; and where the graveyard ends the greensward runs on towards the cathedral and away from its funereal consign-ment. The building soars up effortlessly, solidly, with its great square tower in the middle. But the subtle colour of its masonry – a blush that is vague and variable – and the faint haze through which it is seen, appear to endow it with a sort of weightlessness.

The interior fully lives up to the expectations created by the building's external aspect. It is conducive to prayer, as are cathedrals in our country.* And once more, as much as the proportions and the architectural configuration, it is the colouring which bestows the place with mystique and nobility. Pink, grey, ochre, green, all merge and combine, superimposed one on the other or seen in sequences. And, as with the colours, so it is with the different styles of architecture. All are to be found there, from Norman to late Perpendicular. But where the Norman imprint is most visible in Chester is in the church of St. John, a very fine example, expertly restored, of the simple, solemn, solid architecture produced in that early period. Contemplating the great girth and the robustness of those columns, you appreciate something significant: that the Normans were often rapacious and destructive, but they could, when they chose to, build upon indestructible foundations, and that their presence is felt in the origins or at the base of everything or almost everything in England.

Centuries earlier, however, this country had undergone invasion by another great conquering people, and vestiges of the Roman occupation are readily found in Chester. For four centuries Deva, the camp on the Dee, was the headquarters of the famous Twentieth Legion. In the garden next to the Water Tower there are remains of Roman columns, arches and hypocausts; and one of the towers of the Castle – Norman, in

---

*   Notable in this respect are the recommendations made *To the Pilgrim Visitor*: '*Look* and you will see many beautiful things. / *Read* and you will learn many things fit to be known. / *Find* your special chapel or corner. / *Pray* on your knees, somewhere, for a while. / *May* the peace of God be with you.'

In the nearby church of St. John one finds these other recommendations: 'Whoever you are / who enters into this / Church, / Remember / it is the House of God: / Be reverent. / Be silent. / Be meditative. / Be humble.'

fact – still bears the name of Julius Caesar's Tower.

16 March

Time to leave Chester. Evening is drawing in, leaden but gentle. In the middle distance, square fields marked out by hedges and clumps of trees make a soothing vista from the moving train. The naked trees form a sort of misty tracery in the undulating countryside. Beyond Chester the horizon broadens out. Single oak trees, seen from a distance, seem to merge together as thick copses. The Welsh mountains, looming into sight, look close enough to reach out and touch. Are those ruined castles that one can see on the tops? The farmland becomes softer, gently rolling. Cows. Small farm-houses. A man and a woman on horseback go by. He wears a high hat, red jacket and white jodhpurs; she has on a bowler hat, a light grey outfit with split skirt. They must come from that big house, standing serenely on the high ground over there, white with black-painted timbers. The horses are sprightly, graceful, appearing to be highly strung even. The occasional thatched cottage appears. The occasional nest high up in a tree, or, suddenly, a lot all together, bulky and straggly. Field after field after field. – Crewe: dark fog, engines, smoke. And, picked out in the darkness, the white lettering on the wagons: Loco-coal, L.M.S.

London, 17 March

How I missed seeing the final game in the Home Nations competition, England vs. Scotland. – I took a very early lunch and set off. The weather in the afternoon was splendid. I had two hours to spare, but still had to obtain a ticket. My calculations were: one hour to get to the football stadium; a short time queuing (assuming I wasn't one of the first there); a short time taking in the spectacle of the ground filling up, and then, finally, the big match. I could get there by underground, by train or by bus. The underground – I reckoned – is the surest way of arriving on time, but perhaps I'd arrive too early and, more important, I'd miss the London sightseeing to be had by travelling on the bus. In fact there was a bus stop opposite the tube station. If my bus did not turn up before too long, I'd just go underground and make up the lost time.

I waited for ages. Just as I was about to give up, along it came. I got on board with some misgivings. These disappeared when, Baedekker in hand, I was tracing our route along unknown London streets. But they soon came back again when suburban monotony started to devour the minutes with insatiable voracity. And misgivings turned into anxiousness when it was no longer minutes that were being gobbled up but whole quarters of an hour. And this mood turned into one of distress when (probably not far from our destination) the accumulation of vehicles caused a traffic jam, and the traffic jam devoured my last remaining hope, patience and time. Trapped inside the glass-paned big box-on-wheels, unable to move forwards or backwards, unable to take any decision of my own to escape from the impasse, condemned to sit it out until the congestion untangled itself, I cursed – with the usual degrading futility of this not untypical reaction – my earlier keenness to put in some urban sightseeing. Anyway, by the time I alighted from the bus there was barely a quarter of an hour to go before kick-off. The shred of hope that still sustained me was failing and fading by the second: all those people heading in the opposite direction from mine, where else could they be coming from, except from the stadium, disappointed already? Perhaps there would be ticket touts, I thought to myself in a final appeal to whatever produces lucky breaks.

There was nobody selling tickets outside the ground. The turnstiles were closed: no more spectators were being admitted. The immense terraces were overflowing. Groups of people were scurrying in all directions hoping still to find a turnstile open. I joined them. To no avail. At each entrance there was a subdued and dejected mass of humanity, waiting and hoping against hope.

I went back to the main gate. I simply could not believe that all was lost. Some policemen cleared a way through the people gathered there: they were bustling along a couple of men they had arrested. One of these, smartly dressed, respectable-looking, tall and well-built, was trying to convince a policeman that it was all a mistake. He was pale, gasping, although forcing a smile. They disappeared from view, followed by a few nosey-parkers who were no doubt looking for some compensation in that bit of drama. Suddenly, there it was, not far away from me, the fleeting apparition of something red, a ticket. A little man was offering it for sale. Everybody around was looking at it greedily. Some were asking how much? But nobody was buying. 'Seven shillings,' I thought I heard, and I pushed my way forward.

'Alright,' I said, after taking a quick look at the ticket, and I proffered him a ten-shilling note.

'Oh, no!' said the little man.

'How much is it, then?'

'Seventeen shillings.'

No. To pay seven shillings for a ticket priced at less than three was not out of the question. But seventeen! At that moment, the principle of not being taken for a ride, of not being the 'country cousin', counted more for me than any other consideration. I confess too that my impulsiveness was now being restrained by a certain unease: the fact that there were no ticket touts to be seen meant that it was forbidden. Perhaps I was on the point of committing a 'crime' (for the English any slight mis-demeanour is a crime). And who was to say whether those two unfortunates we had seen being accompanied to the police station had committed no other infringement than being the seller and the buyer of a ticket like the one offered to me? The English deal with these matters very strictly. And there was no shortage of policemen in our immediate vicinity.

Soon, though, all my worry about being duped or about falling foul of the law disappeared, to be replaced by a more powerful feeling: I had been a fool. Being offered the rare opportunity to repair the results of my miscalculation, the rare opportunity to watch an exceptional football match, I had made a pathetic mess of it. This was really where I had allowed myself to be cheated: to avoid being done out of a few shillings, I had let myself be done out of a tremendous spectacle the likes of which I should probably never again have the opportunity to see.

I looked to see if I could find the little man again. Perhaps he had not yet sold the ticket. Perhaps he had more. But he had disappeared. For a moment I thought I had found him.

'It wasn't you who offered me a ticket a while ago?'

'No: but, if you want, I know a man who has some and I can get you one.'

'Fine: let's go.'

'No. Give me a pound and I'll fetch it for you.'

'No, thank you.'

Did I look so stupid? I gave it up as a bad job. There were still groups of people outside the entrance. A few men had climbed to the top of a tree and were now looking towards the pitch. Could they see anything of the game? Surely not. They could probably see a tiny bit more than what I could see from down at street level: just a few spectators at the top of the highest terrace, and nothing else. From observing their reactions I might just be able to follow vaguely what was going on in the game. One has to accept things as they are!

And this mood of positive resignation gradually took over. I had not wasted the afternoon completely. I shall never know what it is like to watch the final of the Home Nations competition; but, on the other hand, I shall have found out what it is like to miss it, while being just a stone's-throw away from where the match is being played. And from the point of view of true knowledge, I should not like to say which one is the richer experience.

18 March

Morning in Hyde Park. – Reminiscences of Barcelona's Passeig de Gràcia, spring sunshine, ladies wearing a lot of make-up, some gentlemen – young and old – in top hats. A variegated and cosmopolitan assemblage: so diverse that it did not create an unmistakably English impression. People who see only London do not get to know the true England.

London, 20 March

I am tempted to think that, in England, the hotels where you find the best food are the Temperance Hotels.

Vevey, Switzerland, 23 April

What insights are to be had into the psychology of peoples and the peculiar genius of different languages, just from public information notices! Waiting for my train, I entertain myself by copying down the following:

> *Les voyageurs ne sont pas appelés avant le départ des trains.*
> *Zum einsteigen in die Züge wird nicht gerufen.*
> *Non si anuncia la partenza dei treni.*
> *No calling out for trains.*

And on board the train:

Alarm signal	*Signal d'alarme*
To stop the train,	*Pour faire arrêter le train en*
pull down the chain.	*cas de danger, tirer la chaine.*
Penalty for improper	*Défense de s'en server sans*
use £5.	*motif sous peine d'une*
	amende de £5.

Paris, 23 April, Night

Vevey-Paris. – Entering the compartment I felt as though I was back in England: it was occupied by five English women, the windows were part-opened, pleasantly letting in the cool air, and their voices glided between them in a sort of whisper. The most interesting member of the group was the monumental, extravagant older lady – mother, grandmother or aunt of the rest? – with a tall hat resting over her eyes, gold-rimmed glasses perched on her nose, as she reclined comfortably in her corner, with the table unfolded before her on which she played endlessly at solitaire, for five hours without a break, every imaginable kind of solitaire. For her there was no countryside and no conversation, no Vaud country and no Burgundy land, no daughters or nieces. There was just that pack of French playing cards which she was laying out one by one, brightly coloured and with suggestive designs, until the table was covered by them. I am sure that for her the great charm of any journey was just this: playing games of solitaire. The same games she plays in her 'cosy corner' at home, but played now on board the Orient Express, or in a hotel at a height of 2,000 metres, or on a little steamer plying across a placid lake. And, when all is said and done, if we were to dig deep down into the hearts of many travellers, would we perhaps not discover that the pleasure they derive from their journeys is, more or less, just like that good lady's, a pleasure which, at first sight, might strike us as odd? Eating, drinking, sleeping, laughing, feeling, loving, everything they do within their familiar horizon, but done far away from home, in exceptional and unknown places. And in my own case, stamped as a writer, do I not derive one of the richest delights of my wanderings from the writing itself – or from imagining what I will or would write – in foreign surroundings?

24 April, a.m.

Paris–Calais. – A French couple, newly-weds, since probably just the day before. Shiny new wedding rings. Nothing passionate, but obvious tenderness. He even has a slight lisp: greyish hair, sombre clothes, smart but modestly so. The woman has attractive features, but is anaemic-looking, a peaches-and-cream complexion. Her voice is very sweet, and slow.

From a hamper they take out their lunch: hard-boiled eggs, a meat pie. An appetising aroma spreads through the compartment. They each have their own cutlery. They share what is left of a bottle of champagne, spilling a little of it.

'*Hier, à table,*' she says.

'*Mais non,*' he insinuates.

'*Mais oui,*' she insists, still looking at him, smiling with a look of benevolent, affectionate superiority. And she goes on:

'*Mais oui; pourquoi pas?*'

A few crumbs from the pie have fallen on the floor.

'*Enlevez-moi ces saletés,*' she orders, in the same very gentle tone.

What a difference between them and the man (a Bulgarian?) sitting next to them, chewing a cigar he has not been allowed to smoke, and who watches them sternly, with a hint of vindictive cruelty. (A hard, podgy face, tight brow, grey hair curling out from beneath his wide-brimmed hat.) He is reflecting on all the calamities – as though he could foresee them – which will come down on the two of them, today so happy, and which will be attracted especially by her fragility: illnesses, difficult child-births, torment from the children, financial worries, conjugal rifts, unfaithfulness from the husband.

They have with them all sorts of newspapers:

'*Quel journal préférez-vous?*'

'*Celui que vous ne voudrez pas.*'

'*Vous avez mal?*'

'*Toujours au foie.*'

'*Mais pas la tête?*'

'*Non.*'

Long discussion on where they should stand the half-bottle of Evian water. Eventually they find a place for it: on the travel rug.

'That's where you should have put the champagne as well. On its side. Don't you know that champagne should always be laid on its side, because of the gas?... Make sure you chew that banana properly.'

The husband does tend to go on about things. They will make an extremely punctilious *ménage*. He will lose his temper from time to time. She will twist him round her little finger.

London, 24 April, evening

Is there not perhaps some slight exaggeration in the bad reputation of the English Channel? I should certainly think so, if I were to judge from my own experience, and even from the testimony of some other travellers. This has been the seventh time that I have made the crossing. Occasionally the sea was as smooth as the most tranquil lake can ever be. At other times the swell was very slight. Only once was the crossing rather rough, but only moderately so and I was affected by just the initial symptoms of sea-sickness. And today the crossing was splendid. I would be wary, however, about making generalisations from my own experience and about detracting from the reputation that weighs upon the waters of the Channel. On the contrary: I like to imagine the reputation to be true, and that the waves have been calmed on my account.

London, 25 April, a.m.

'Safety first' advice is at odds with the haste shown by bus-conductors to get their passengers, even female ones, to alight while the vehicle is still moving. It must be said that all London women are very adept at getting on and off buses. I shall always remember how, on the second day of my first visit to London, before I became aware of the vertiginous speed that those buses reach almost as soon as they set off, I was about to board one. It came past me with such a whoosh that I thought better of it. A few metres further on (with the bus going even faster) a tall, slim, fashionable girl stepped onto it, with an extremely elegant jump and follow-through. I felt rather vexed. But, I confess, I have never had any inclination to imitate her.

Oxton, 25 April, evening

I arrive in Oxton after a pleasant journey, sunny and warm. Between Vevey and Chester the whole world is in bloom. But beyond Chester, neither sunshine nor flowers in bloom. As I get used again to being back there, I find that Birkenhead now looks even uglier, darker and dirtier. But even so there is still something attractive about the place.

27 April

The Empire. – When I first arrived in London I found accommodation in one of the innumerable boarding houses in Gower Street, not far from University College. Even closer by was the 'Indian Students' Union'. There was a constant movement in and out of students with their darkly yellowish faces, slightly wild eyes and pale lips. To round off the European dress which they wore – predominantly grey, bell-bottomed Oxford bags – several preferred not to go bare-headed like the other students but rather to parade, with a rather fierce pride, an Indian turban. Some female students were dressed from head to foot in a special costume that I imagined was more or less traditional: I recall a combination of yellow skirts with a brownish bodice, white shoes and stockings and a sort of scarf on their heads.

That was the Empire.

Going out of my boarding house, in the street outside, I stopped in front of a large advertisement. It was a publicity poster for emigration to Australia. On one side there was an image of the deprived, overcrowded and grim living conditions in the dark English cities: the other side showed leisure, liberty and prosperity for the same people transported to the wide-open spaces of Australia. Now the man was driving powerful machinery, working the responsive and wealth-giving land; the woman, her face no longer showing any sign of illness or of grinding poverty, dressed in shorts and high boots, was suckling a sturdy pink child. Later, a similar advertisement, this time in a newspaper, likewise encouraging emigration to Australia with hyperbolic and stirring invocations of liberty and wealth, moved somebody to comment within my ear-shot:

'Yes, but when they get there they find that the reality of life "down under" is very different.'

No matter: that was the Empire too.

A little further from my lodgings, turning a corner, I found myself opposite the British Museum. Inside, once again, I encountered the Empire, but this time in all its imposing vastness. All the four corners of the earth, methodically pillaged, had supplied the biggest part, the most valuable part, of the contents of that museum which is one of the foremost in the world.

A short time later, I became acquainted with the Empire through a port and its traffic – one of the most telling forms in which dynamic imperial expansion can make itself known. The port of Liverpool, the most important in England in terms of tonnage of registered vessels and export volume, surpassing London (which has, however, a greater volume of imports), is a living, powerful evocation of Empire. Manufactured goods, cotton products made in the Manchester area, coal from Wales and salt from Cheshire, these are the main exports; raw cotton, cereals and other products from the United States or the Empire constitute the basic imports. From the great docks of Liverpool vessels sail for Ireland, Canada, India, Africa, China, the West Indies, South America.

That, that was the Empire.

But, when I moved away from the port and the ships crowding it, the imperial vision disappeared almost completely. At the University here were perhaps no more than half a dozen coloured students. English people from Lancashire and Cheshire, together with a high proportion of Welshmen, made up the student body. One day, however, not far from the University, I met the Empire head on. Walking along near to me was a thin young man, of olive complexion, with dark, moist eyes, rather feverish-looking. Something about him told you that he had the sea in his background. I had the impression that he was keen to talk to me, and out of curiosity I slowed down. He just wanted a match. But I was intrigued by what nationality he might be, unable to work it out. He mentioned the name of an island, I now forget which.

'It's French,' I said with much uncertainty.

'It used to be,' he smiled in reply, 'but the English…'

He did not finish the sentence: a semi-circular sweep of his arm, like that of a croupier pulling in the winnings, evoked more eloquently than could any words the transfer of the island to English dominion.

Yes, indeed. That also was the Empire: a lucky strike, a smart move when the time is ripe, and one more island goes to England, the banker in this casino. And then, let the game recommence.

As I did not go to the port every day and as I did not meet every day islanders from afar who had become imperial British subjects, this Empire would not have impinged on my consciousness except in the form of tinned fruits and the signboards of some specialised grocers. I would not have been aware of it, that is, if a great propaganda campaign had not suddenly been launched to promote Empire produce through a series of special advertisements. One day, all the way along my usual route through town I kept seeing a coloured poster and then another one, all very well produced, showing a gallery of 'Empire Builders', starting with John Cabot and Sir Francis Drake, the great English seafarer presented in Spanish manuals of history as nothing but an atrocious pirate. The figures in that most impressive line of men of action were crowned with the slogan 'Empire Building'.

After that there appeared periodically a new poster in the series. Each of these presented a different aspect of the Empire, especially with reference to the range of its products. And what a vast Empire it is! One day we saw the cotton-fields of Sudan: green plains with splashes of white, bright tents, shimmering sunshine, shiny black skins, long-suffering camels. 'Trade in the Empire is growing,' said the caption. 'The Empire can clothe itself.' And this was confirmed by figures relating to production in South Africa.

Another day it was all the foodstuffs exported by the different countries of the Empire: cheese from Canada, tea from Ceylon, eggs from Ireland, New Zealand butter, Australian lamb, and so on and so forth. 'The Empire is your Garden,' affirmed the caption. 'Empire vitamins,' said the tiny label on a packet carried by a sprightly, smiling old fellow shown coming out of a grocer's: 'Wealth? Health? Long life? Empire foods!'

Then it was the turn of the paddy-fields in Burma, stretching as far as the eye could see, glittering in the sun. Carts, pulled by oxen with enormous horns, piled high. 'Burma is the world's major producer of rice.' '1,300,000,000 tons per year.' Just imagine how many rice puddings can be made with all that rice! But, no need to rack one's brain working it out; the poster itself will tell us: 32,000,000,000 rice puddings.[18] There cannot be many parts of the world that are as precious for England as Burma.

18   It has proved difficult to square accurately the characteristics of the various series of posters mentioned with the author's evocation of them here. The numbers relating to rice production and rice puddings certainly seem incongruous.

I will not continue with this evocation of the British Empire suggested through an unending series of thought-provoking posters. But I am loath to omit mention of one of these aimed at whetting English appetites with an account in three pictures of the route to the Indies: a ship standing off the Rock of Gibraltar, the same vessel going through the Suez Canal and finally shown again approaching Bombay. Here the city shines brightly, off-white in the background, across the blue waters; a young English couple, both dressed in white, are looking out towards it, leaning against the ship's railing. The British spirit, so steeped in travel, must have been stirred many times before this white city, the enormous gateway to 'Enormous, captivating India'.

Christmas came. Could imperial propaganda miss the opportunity to form an association between the Empire, its produce and the festivities so firmly tied to English sentimentality? No, it could not. A few days before the holiday began, the Christmas posters appeared. I remember a harbour at night, with a mountain close by, everything decked out in bright lights. The captions were more loaded than ever. With great refinement, they wove together incitements to consumption and yuletide sentimentality: 'Home produce crowns Christmas celebrations.' 'A good resolution for the New Year: when shopping, always buy Empire, please.' 'Let the Empire fill your Christmas tree.' 'The Empire is one big family.'

'A Happy New Year to the whole Empire!'

28 April

At the Playhouse, *The Admirable Crichton*. The audience were spell-bound by the dialogue and by the comings and goings of the action. 'Good', 'beautiful', 'splendid' were the comments I overheard among those sitting close to me. I recall that in Barcelona the Catalan version was quite well received, but it had a very short run; in Castilian it was a flop. Diana Winyard won as much admiration from the audience as did the play itself. 'Lovely girl,' said some women in seats close to mine. She did not have, this time, a leading role. But that did not matter: her graceful presence always stands out. I do not know whether it is her talent as an actress that emphasises her beauty or whether it is her beauty that enhances her performance.*

29 April

Around half past six I walked down the lane by the fields. At Oxton Cricket Club they were playing cricket and tennis. A short way further on I sat down. I was looking over towards Oxton, and it was very pretty to see the green of the sports ground and the young people of both sexes, dressed in white, playing there, and, in the background standing among the gardens, the houses of the Liverpool 'gentry', against a gloomy sky, as if a storm were brewing, a sky tinged with faint sunlight just penetrating the haze.

2 May

A Crusade into Catalonia. – Whenever I have in my hands a book with an index of names and places, where there might be a reference however direct or oblique to Catalonia, I feel a perfectly understandable impulse to look there for the name

---

* She has subsequently had a notable career as a cinema actress.

of my homeland. A similar tendency is that which, when consulting the catalogue in a foreign library, makes me wonder whether any Catalan book is listed there and, if so, which one it might be. Thus, for example, four years ago I found that in the library of Lausanne University our literature was represented by the famous presidential speech delivered by Àngel Guimerà to the Barcelona *Ateneu* and by *La mitja taronja* [The Better Half].[19] In the same way I discovered that, two years ago, in the library of the League of Nations, 'national minorities' section, there was still nothing listed relating to our national cause.

Upon enquiring by post whether they did in fact have any material from Catalonia, I received a courteous reply in the affirmative; and in this response there showed through a quite understandable commendatory tone: in their holdings there was, among other publications like those of the official body concerned with the control of malaria, the complete collection of the *Anuaris* of the Institute of Catalan Studies.[20]

In Geneva University library we also found several publications of the Institute (some numbers of the *Anuari*, not all of them), the doctoral thesis by Amadeu Pagès[21] on *Ausias*

19   Guimerà (Tenerife 1845–Barcelona 1924), author principally of drama and public figure influential in the early evolution of modern Catalan nationalism. The other work mentioned is a three-act play (bilingual Catalan/Spanish) by J.M. Arnau, first performed in 1868, published in Barcelona in 1879. Although Soldevila does not say as much, his contemporary readers would have seen something slightly ironic in the conjunction of these two works: the first a resonant declaration of Catalanist principles made by a major literary figure and the second a very minor popular play, produced at a time when public performance exclusively in Catalan was officially prohibited.

20   The Institut d'Estudis Catalans (founded in 1907) is Catalonia's national academy. Its activities became clandestine after the Spanish Civil War, until its official status was restored under the Spanish constitutional dispensation of 1978 and the Catalan Autonomy Statute of 1979. The Anuari referred to is an important component among various collections of academic publications, in all the main fields of learning and science, from the IEC.

21   Pagès (1865–1952), French scholar of Romance philology who edited the first modern edition of poems in Catalan by the major Valencian poet Ausiàs March (1397–1459).

March et ses prédécesseurs, some of the Institute's publications on applied chemistry, as well as *L'Atlàntida* and *Canigó* by Verdaguer. Libraries like the Bibliothèque Nationale
in Paris and that in the British Museum in London have large
holdings of Catalan works or of books relating to Catalonia,
such that all the researchers who have worked there are fully
acquainted with the possibilities offered for specialised study
in the fields of history, literature, archaeology, philology, etc.
The surprises to be had in these great libraries are to do
with more discrete matters. I wrote already (12 April 1927)
about the one bestowed on me the first time I worked in the
British Museum Library, in the form of Guerau de Liost's book
Selvatana amor.

Moving on from the effect of that particular pleasant
surprise, I set to work in earnest. Among the works I consulted
was *Sigil·lografia catalana* by Ferran de Sagarra.[22] They had
only the first volume, and a note in the catalogue indicated
that publication had been interrupted. I explained that this
was not correct.

'Have you seen the second volume?' the librarian asked
me, sceptically.

'You can be sure that I have,' I replied.

'Are you certain?' he said, maintaining his position.

'Absolutely so.'

He made a note of the details. That was over a year ago.
I expect that by now the volume in question will be on their
shelves.

In Liverpool it cannot be said that there is an abundance

22   (1853–1939) Historian. The five volumes (1916–32) of his *Sigil·lografia* are an exhaus-
tive repertory and study of medieval and early-modern official seals.

of Catalan books available, but nor can it be said that there is a shortage of them. In the University Library, known also as the Tate Library, named after the same benefactor who founded the splendid Tate Gallery in London, can be found works by some of our medieval authors and by some modern ones too: among them Llull,[23] the complete works, and *L'Atlàntida* by Verdaguer, standing alongside Mistral.[24] Our historiography is represented there by Víctor Balaguer's[25] *Història de Catalunya*; and among foreign works dealing with our history there is Calmette's *Louis XI, Jean II et la Révolution catalane*, and also *The Rise of the Spanish Empire by R.B. Merriman*. Catalan authors who wrote in Spanish are represented by Boscán, Montcada and Eugeni d'Ors, the latter with his *Oceanografía del tedio*, a Spanish translation of a sequence of short newspaper articles composed originally in Catalan.[26]

23   Ramon Llull (c.1232–c.1315), considered to be the founding father of Catalan litera-ture, the first European to use a vernacular for philosophical writing. His vast production (in Arabic and Latin as well as in Catalan) constructed a system of thought to counter the influence of Islam. Narrative and poetic modes are integrated with his extensive philosophi-cal, devotional and contemplative works.

24   On Verdaguer, see note 11 on pg. 113. Frederic Mistral (1830–1914), writer and prominent figure in the revival of nineteenth-century Occitanian language and culture, the *Félibrige*. He won the Nobel Prize in 1908.

25   Víctor Balaguer (Barcelona 1824–Madrid 1901), politician, historian and writer, very influential in establishing, under Romantic influences, the bases of the nineteenth-century Catalan revival movement.

26   Soldevila is being mischievous here. Eugeni d'Ors (1881–1954) had been an influential writer and thinker in the politico-cultural movement of *Noucentisme* which gave great impetus to Catalan nationalism in the first decades of the twentieth century and laid the foundations for thorough 'normalisation' of the language and its literature. By the early 1920s, however, Ors had been discredited and he decamped to Madrid where he swam with the Spa-nish nationalist tide from then until his death. Like many of his contemporaries, Soldevila's own intellectual and literary formation owed much to *Noucentisme*, and the reticence towards Ors shown here reflects a general attitude among the Catalan intelligentsia following his 'defenestration'.

In the lending library I picked up a work by Rusiñol,[27] I do not now recall which one. And in the catalogue of Picton local library, under the subject heading 'Catalonia', I found a single title: *A Crusade into Catalonia* (Liverpool, 1913), by Hepburn Ballantine.[28]

What we have here is a travel book or, rather, a book about a single expedition, since the author went more or less straight from his home town of Birkenhead to Catalonia, with the sole objective of doing a walking traverse of Andorra and through the neighbouring district of Urgell south of the Pyrenees. He then returned to Birkenhead to write his book which deals almost exclusively with his sojourn in Catalan territory. That was in 1894. Paris, Toulouse, Aix-les-Termes were stages on his way south. When he entered Andorra the first person he met was a poverty-stricken shepherd who addressed him neither as *monsieur* nor as 'master' but as *senyor*. 'His eyes,' says Ballantine, 'were of the most intense blue - blue as the blue aconite which we encountered so often in our wanderings. Not six words of his could we make out, for to him French was as foreign to him as English: we were at last come to where the beautiful and vigorous language of the old troubadours, in its purest survival, is alone current.'

The English traveller offers the shepherd a few centimes to thank him for the directions given, but the shepherd, proudly, will not accept. And Hepburn Ballantine, filled with respect

27   Santiago Rusiñol (1861–1931), painter and writer, was a major figure in the fin-de-siècle movement of Catalan *Modernisme*. The overlapping phase of *Noucentisme* (see note 26) was in large measure a reaction against the perceived vagueness, subjectivity and indiscipline of *modernista* values, in the creative sphere and also in politics. Soldevila's offhand comment here is thus quite loaded.

28   Soldevila mistakenly (but understandably) transcribes Hepburn as 'Helpburn'. See Translator's Perspective, pg. 14.

and admiration, continues on his way. He goes through Canillo, then through Encamp. Everything is a source of wonderment to him. He learns the word *aigua* and notes: 'What a pretty sounding trisyllabic word it is!'[29] He drinks for the first time directly from the conical spout of a *porró* (which he writes as 'puro'), describing it and attributing to it a purpose of moderating consumption. He is far from insensitive towards the prestige of medieval remains and traditions. And he is no less respectful of authority bearing arms. He meets a border guard and, on learning that he has left Andorra and is now in Spain, he stands to attention and declares, 'Spain, I salute thee!' The name of Catalonia moves him deeply: 'The name even of the province,' he writes, 'is like a spell; there is a melancholy cadence in the very sound of Catalunya that is bewitching, and that haunts the heart like the memory of a romance read in childhood.'

Continuing in his naïve admiration and with his ingenuous remarks, he is captivated by how chocolate is taken *à la mode catalane*, that is, by dipping bread in the thick concoction, which he finds 'graceful and comforting', quite unlike the watered-down cocoa he is used to.

The people are kind; the language, beautiful and sonorous. Who dared to say that Catalan is an ugly language? An Englishwoman had averred this a short time previously. And Hepburn rises indignantly to make a blazing defence of our language and the *langue d'oc*, drawing their boundaries, recalling their glories and raising his voice in support of their continued cultivation in literature. And, at the close of

29   The word, meaning 'water', is made up in fact of two syllables: ai-gua.

the book, nostalgia for those days spent wandering through the 'deep valleys that pierce through the heart of Catalonia' prompts him to reproduce the words of Flaubert: '*Il y a des endroits de la terre si beaux qu'on a envie de les serrer contre son coeur.*' And the book ends with a resonant ADÉU.

Ah! Hepburn Ballantine, you of the kindly oval face, of the bushy white whiskers hiding your mouth like a thick veil, of the gentle but slightly mischievous look,[30] if you were still alive today, I would go to your sad suburb in the dark city of Birkenhead and I would shake you warmly by the hand.

9 May

To Chester to see the horse racing. When buying my ticket at Birkenhead station, the clerk, who knows me from seeing me nearly every day, but who had never said anything to me, smiled with a hint of excitement and said: 'Are you going to the races?' And he looked to me like a docile prisoner who, from behind his bars, was wistfully watching people going at liberty to enjoy themselves and to have fun, while he managed just from the sight of them to participate a little in their enjoyment.

In Chester the streets were thronged and the race-track packed full. A delightful sight: the vast expanse of turf, the River Dee, clumps of tall trees with thick foliage, the city walls – now streaming with people – the railway, a red train going past, then a green one.

I place a bet on *Nevermore* and then see that I have backed a winner: it was the name, the name alone that caught my eye.

30   An elegant evocation of the photogravure portrait which is the frontispiece to the extremely rare edition (privately published) of Ballantine's book.

But the good fellow who is supposed to give me my winnings (one of the innumerable bookmakers installed on the course) seems to want to do me out of them. I put him and his conscience to the test, watching as he is paying out everybody else. I stand there motionless, without insistently claiming aloud what is due to me. It is clear that he is most reluctant to pay up. My interest increases; no longer is it a matter of his clear conscience being at stake in the stand-off with me, for I am now in the position of being a judge in the dispute, and I feel that at stake also is the honour of Great Britain itself. A short time goes by. I make a slight movement as though to walk away. And then immediately he hands over the money. There are three sides to the satisfaction I enjoy: I have my winnings, this man has triumphed over evil, and the honour of Great Britain has been saved.

Another race: the jockeys flash past in dizzying, many-hued array. 'St. Mary's Kirby!' shrieks a woman standing behind me, waving her betting-slip. 'One pound!' I turn round and see that the voice proclaiming to the four winds the name of the winning horse and the profit it has brought has come from behind a halo of white hair. I looked out of mere curiosity, but that was enough to cause a reaction of embarrassment in the lady: she composed herself immediately, fell silent and adopted a demeanour befitting her age. Today I seem to have acquired some strange ability, without opening my mouth, to make people recover their sense of dignity.

Tea is served. A bevy of waitresses emerges from the catering vans. Trays are passed down to them: biscuits, sweet pastries, cakes, and the ladies spread out in every direction across the spectators' enclosures. Walker's Warrington Ales have a large marquee, with a long bar. Bottles of beer are served up quickly. No glasses: drunk straight from the bottle. Once empty, the bottles are thrown on the ground: they are everywhere, glinting in the daylight.

In one corner, a man in a bowler hat is sitting on the ground. In front of him is a sort of chessboard. He is all the time encouraging people to have a go: 'Everybody plays, and everybody wins!' Only one person falls for this, though: a young man who has hardly any hair, as though because of some secret illness. He wears a light-coloured summer suit, but it is dirty and shabby. Pennies are thrown on to the board: any coin not landing on a black square is lost (which is what happens almost every time); a shilling is won for each coin landing on the black. Penny after penny, uninterruptedly, our gambler is aiming at the board. Penny after penny the man in the bowler hat rakes them into his bag. Every coin lands on a white square, and even the odd one which has landed on black is whisked with the little rake into the bag, perhaps because he is so used to winning. Does the man playing kick up a fuss? No: the slip is simply pointed out in a polite way, with no raising of the voice, and it is put right immediately.

I leave the racecourse. A tram takes me further away from town, through leafy suburbs. The houses are very small, tiny: all with their little front gardens lined with ivy. One can see into these houses between their flimsy white curtains: tables are set for the frugal evening meal. Could anything other than happiness be at home in these unaffected interiors, on such a perfect May day, sheltered by the trees and under the changing blueness of the sky at this late hour?

Manchester, 12 May

The final of the Lancashire Cup. Chastened by what happened to me at the England-Scotland game, I leave myself so much time that I arrive at the Old Trafford ground an hour before the Manchester United–Bury match begins. The stadium is empty, but people are beginning to turn up: 'Very dull day' is heard, here and there, among them. The sky is leaden, but there is no fog, not even a mist. The ground is surrounded by smoking factories. The grass pitch has a sort of scoured appearance.

The terraces and stands fill up quickly. The bandsmen are here, playing their instruments as they march to their place in the centre of the pitch. They are led by a haughty-looking character, in his uniform, with a black feather on top of his hat, and with a long mace which he swings and twirls, very full of himself. Then he holds it straight out in front of him. When the band marches off, he gives an even more exaggerated display. He has one of those moustaches that are sometimes seen, especially among the police: very small, very thin, waxed and twirled at the ends – grotesque.

Now it is time for the championship cup and the replica trophies to be displayed. They are exhibited in the middle of the pitch. Photographs are taken of them, and they too are paraded in front of the crowd.

The game begins. I observe that people do a lot of shouting, but for the most part this consists of natural exclamations: 'goal!', 'hand-ball', etc. The shouting does not go on all the time and it comes in particular from people who have come in through the turnstiles and who are not seated. Sometimes the referee receives his share of abuse. The spectators in my part of the ground make hardly any noise at all. The game does not seem to me particularly rough, but even so three Manchester players have needed attention. Nor is the play at all eye-catching; rather slow; long passing is the prevailing pattern, with only exceptionally the odd short pass. It does not compare with the excitement of our big matches. Manchester won (3-1) because of the indecisiveness and clumsiness of the Bury centre-forward, who missed two chances to make it a draw. And also because of the influence of the crowd, who shouted at him a lot while they barely applauded good play by the other side.

When the game is nearly over, the crowd begins to surge towards where we are: it is here that the presentation of the cup will be performed. The police have to form a chain, by linking arms, in order to hold back the heaving force of so many bodies. There is a kind of undulation, a flux and reflux of innumerable heads. The players are lifted off their feet in victory, freeing themselves as best they can. The captain climbs up to the podium. A man in a white suit makes an address which nobody can hear. The captain gives a short speech of thanks. Then they put a warm coat around his shoulders. The cheering resounds. Close to me some shorthand reporters are exchanging their notes. The chimneys continue to belch out smoke, quietly, into the murky sky.

14 May

The English like giving names, as it were 'officially', to things which in other countries do not merit even a popular designation. It happens with trains: The Night Scotsman, The Ulster Express,

The Irish Mail, The Royal Scot… The latter – London, Edinburgh, Glasgow – is moreover advertised as 'The world's longest non-stop run'.

20 May

The weather is quite wintry. The greenness of the leaves is what prevents them from looking desolate.

25 May

One of the most productive activities that the students engage in are the debating sessions which they hold periodically. It strikes me that this intellectual pursuit serves a useful purpose in their education. There is a Chairman or Speaker, then the 'proposer' and the 'opposer' each with his or her respective 'seconders'. The subject and details of the session are announced in advance. A wide variety of topics are debated, some of them rather provocative. Yesterday the female students held a debate on the proposal 'That the university male is a degenerate creature.' They are not 'creatures', one of the speakers said, but overgrown parasites. Proof of this is in the cutlery and other items stolen by them from the refectory. They spend all their time playing games of chance and chatting up the girls. They neglect their studies. In formal university ceremonies they would drown out the voice of the member of staff, who spoke on behalf of the whole institution. They are too effeminate. And the case continued in this less than flattering tone.

27 May

Sunday afternoon. A small park adjoining Liverpool cathedral, close to the cemetery. On a bench, a young man reading. On the bench opposite, a couple: the man is unhealthily pale, bow-legged, with a hair-style resembling that of a medieval monk; his head is resting on the shoulder of the woman, who is skinny, anaemic, meek; two shy and deprived beings in love, each shoring up the other. A scrawny man with a rickety child is giving bread to a starving cat. The heat is oppressively sweltering. Sparrows flutter about in the dust, trying to cool themselves. The cathedral looms high over the scene, indifferent, pinkish red.

29 May

Punctuality. – Punctuality has been considered an eminently Anglo-Saxon virtue. 'British punctuality' is an expression used in just the same way as one might speak of 'mathematical precision'. Be this as it may, my own observations lead me to conclude that, if the reputation does derive from a solid reality, this reality is beginning to show symptoms of splintering. Are these symptoms to be grouped with others which might lead to suspicion about whether in England there is, on the whole, a certain tendency towards decline? Older people make no bones about it, and the topic has even been the subject of opinion polls in the press here: 'Is Britain decadent?'

The symptoms regarding punctuality first came to my notice when observing behaviour among the student population. If the observation had been limited to my own classes I would have felt obliged to seek other causes for failure to turn up on time. But it is quite usual to see, throughout the day, well after the times that classes should officially have begun, students of both sexes in a hurry rushing up and down university staircases. Sometimes also there is a young lecturer among their number. Such a thing, in view of the proverbial English punctuality, ought not to happen. The young people themselves must be aware that they are at fault – an awareness inculcated in the home and at school – because all the late-comers apologise when they come in: 'I am sorry, Sir.'

Setting aside these instances, by no means negligible in themselves, I have been impressed on the whole by evidence of punctuality. In general, in all branches of public services. We can take as an example the tram on which I frequently travel. It runs past our house every ten minutes, but with such strict regularity that I can go out to catch it as time-tabled, just as though it were a train. Also notable is the punctuality with which public entertainment events begin. And an outstanding example is the sight to be seen, around nine o'clock in the morning, in hotel dining-rooms, full of people at breakfast, smartly dressed and ready to go out into the world. Observing the later arrivals, those who turn up between 9.15 and 10 o'clock, we can affirm that they are not English.

But I have found the most impressive examples of all from among the ladies who run boarding houses. Their precision attains such a high degree that I have sometimes suspected they might work on it as a way of impressing foreigners. In our house Mrs. B, as soon as the hands of the clock showed one o'clock pm or eight o'clock in the evening (lunch-time and dinner-time respectively), the gong would sound and the meal was on the table. The slightest delay on our part – the time taken to close my books and to wash my hands – meant that the proprietress would already be getting nervous and would greet us with a stern face. On one such occasion I asked if she would kindly sound the gong two or three minutes before meal-times, because sometimes, absorbed in my work, unaware of how close the appointed hour was, the grave metallic call to table used to take me by surprise and in no position to heed it straight away. She would have none of this. She must have considered that her obligation was only to call me to the dining-room and not to give me notice to stop working.

Here, on the very stroke of the hour to eat, the door opens and in comes the first course, still steaming. I do observe, however, that the spirit of this exactness is the mother, an old lady who is ancien régime through and through. Her daughters are incapable of displaying the same strict punctuality. I record this detail, along with my observations from the university, to the credit of the older English generations and to the detriment of the younger ones. I do so, however, with the expectation that when the latter do take over the running of the house they will rediscover ancestral inflexibility in all matters concerning punctuality.

If this proves to be the case, there is nothing to fear. And meanwhile, while ladies formed in the old school of running an establishment are still in charge, the same can be said. Any inclination to delay or inconformity will be repressed: the family timetable, maintained by womenfolk with as much pertinacity as might be dedicated to keeping alive a sacred flame, will prevent any lasting break with normality. But if the old school gives way, if they go along the route taken by their counterparts in other countries, the proverbial British punctuality will become a mere memory or one of those clichés which are perpetuated through inertia without responding to any objective reality.

1 June

At the Playhouse, *The Claimant* by Watts. One of the characters is a ridiculous caricature of a Spanish woman: she bellows when she summons the servants; she laughs loudly in great guffaws which make her whole body heave; she speaks at the top of her voice, with her mouth full; she sucks her fingers; she is convinced that she is incredibly beautiful. All this notwithstanding, when the actress playing the part came on stage disguised as a typical Spanish *manola*, an old gentleman sitting close to me began to applaud. Nobody joined in. But I wonder what innermost fibres were made to vibrate, what memories or what distant illusions were stirred in the old man of the North by that sudden evocative apparition.

3 June

Marvellous weather. 'Good English weather', as it is known. There is the combination of the large trees in all their late-springtime pomp, the crystal-clear sky and the fresh, invigorating air.

6 June

My third visit to Chester. I spent a long time in the park next to Bonewaldesthorne's Tower – one of the towers on the city wall which is of a remarkable colour, hues of green and reddish violet. Tennis and bowls were being played. My memories of bowling were full of noise and rapid action, the harsh sound of the bowls as they hit asphalt or clattered into one another. And a particular memory from further back, from childhood: the sound comes to me now muffled by distance and by the sand of a garden in summer: I can hear the voices; I can hear the noise of the bowls colliding or hitting the bricks around the edge of the playing area. But all this is now vaguely disturbing to me: present on the occasion were some marvellous female figures. Did I have the same feeling then? Or do I have it only now? Here, on the other hand, such peace and quiet! Is there anything more peaceful than these bowls, the colour of tortoise-shell, sliding gently, slowly, over the smoothness of the closely cropped grass? They themselves seem to experience and to savour deeply the contact with the green as they roll tranquilly over it. 'Just a little further, just a little further,' they seem to be saying to one another, and then they come to a standstill with a kind of contemplative languor. And what of the men who play bowls? I should love to be able to find their enthusiasm for the game, to be able to play it with their combination of concentration and simple good-heartedness. But this would be impossible for me, and has been for a long time. I would have a painful sensation of wasting my time. And this is surprising: to play the game like they do would make me feel this way, whereas to do even less than they do – not even playing, just watching them play – has no such effect. Quite the opposite: I think that I have rarely made better use of my time than doing just this.

*

I walked along the bank of the river. I would have liked to take a trip on one of the little cruisers. At the landing-stage I asked about their timetable, but I was out of luck. As I was walking away I was approached by a young man who spoke to me in French:

'Do you like England?' he said.

'Yes, greatly.' I replied.

'More than France?' he persisted. 'It is winter all year long here,' he chimed in without awaiting my reply.

'Not really: you are exaggerating.'

'Oh no, I am not.'

'I think you are.'

'I am telling you that I am not…'

And we went on like this for a while, until he exclaimed:

'Exaggerating, am I? Just look!'

A big black cloud had appeared from nowhere. It suddenly started to rain hard, so I sheltered under some trees. Two young women (with rain drops settled on their hair like pearls) were laughing hysterically. The shelter soon became inadequate in the torrential downpour. I ran all the way to the tram stop, arriving there out of breath, soaked to the skin… Perhaps the fellow at the landing-stage knew what he was talking about.

It is now around half-past nine and I am in bed. If I imagine that it is about half-past two in the afternoon, it could be the end of a winter's day. It has to be said that the combination of this sky with the slate roofs makes a gloomy picture. This is in spite of all the open space there is here, the gardens and the expensive houses!

6 June

Some time ago M.O.[31] wrote to me expressing how ill at ease he felt. Neither his newspapers from Catalonia nor letters from there were being delivered: he was feeling terribly isolated. I informed him that *La Publicitat*[32] had been temporarily shut down. 'As for correspondence,' I told him, 'do not be surprised: in our country there are many people who are incapable not only of maintaining a proper correspondence but even of replying to a single letter.'

These words of mine might perhaps sound exaggerated. They are, nevertheless, the product of a personal experience which is now long enough to allow me to make certain generalisations on the matter. During the last five years my sojourns in Barcelona have been consistently brief and very exceptional: my relations with friends living there have had to be maintained, almost invariably, through use of the post. This has enabled me to reach a number of conclusions, generally unfavourable ones, regarding the epistolary habits of my fellow countrymen. There are, to be sure, some individuals among them who can keep up a correspondence; but it has to be admitted that they are the exception. And so, when for whatever reason one of them stops sending letters, the sense of isolation to which M.O. referred is produced. There is too the curious feature that the people who are always quick to talk or write about *courtesy*, *correct behaviour* and so on are no better at keeping up a proper correspondence than the vast majority. The opposite is

31   Marçal Olivar (Barcelona 1900–94): Catalan literary scholar, art historian and translator. He was lector in Spanish at the University of Glasgow (1928–30).

32   See footnote 1 of the *Introductory note to the 1938 edition*

sometimes the case; some who have a reputation for being discourteous and not very communicative are the ones who exchange letters in the way that good manners require.

The phenomenon we are discussing may have several explanations. First of all, among writers in Catalan, there is the over-work which affects many of them. After a good number of hours of writing every day, as I well know from my own experience, it is sometimes irksome to have to pick up the pen again and return to putting words on paper, even just a few lines. This excuse deserves to be taken into account, but it does mean that in our country a lot of writers are appearing on the scene who would benefit from having a secretary. The phenomenon, though, is not limited to the literary sector and it is encountered every time one needs to write a letter on mundane business. This means that we need to think what other causes there might be.

Perhaps one of the most important of them is this: we Catalans in general have not really understood that not to reply to a letter is just as much a demonstration of discourtesy and bad manners as is not responding to a direct oral question. The result is that many people take a quite lackadaisical attitude towards answering letters. A letter is an item of no importance. On several occasions I have received after months of delay ones which had been eventually forwarded to me from centres which already had a record of my home address. A letter could have been lying for days and days on a desk or in a drawer, waiting for somebody to do something about putting it back in the post.

Perhaps another cause could be the fact that many people in our country still have not taken on board the possibility and the acceptability of writing short letters, of just three or four lines. For them a letter is a mountain which has to be laboriously climbed, instead of their seeing it as a tiny hill that can be got over in a few strides.

And then there is the question of the practical advantages, of the benefits in terms of time, convenience and economy that can be derived from well established letter-writing habits. We are not referring here to situations where big distances are involved; we are talking now specifically about short distances: within the same city, for example. In five minutes you have written your letter; just work out the time you lose if you go in person to convey by word of mouth the same thing to your addressee. Combine all these advantages with being able to send by post parcels and packets of all kinds, and you will have a product which loses out only to use of the telephone – and not in every single case.

The laxness of our habits in this sphere of activity (while there are peoples in the Iberian Peninsula whose slackness surpasses ours) is visible, especially, when contrasted with the regular and punctual epistolary activity in more advanced countries. It is marvellous to see how in England letters are replied to immediately by ordinary people. With the distances involved being so short, it is not at all unusual, quite normal rather, to receive your reply the following day or inside two days. The fact is that the English not only answer letters but they do not leave correspondence in abeyance either: a laudable habit, the first which must be acquired in order to achieve perfection in this matter. Naturally, I am not speaking of long-term, sustained correspondences, in which a certain rhythm is necessary. Nor am I speaking of letters to which a response is optional. Nor do I have in mind – it goes without saying – letters which do not deserve any reply.

It could be that someone who is reading this now might mutter: 'Just look who is talking!' I am not sure if the charge sticks; but I ask my hypothetical reader to reflect that anybody can have a memory lapse. He must also reflect that the unanswered letter, perhaps, still has not come into my hands. The point is that I have perhaps on the odd occasion failed to reply to a letter, but that this is not a habit in me.

7 June

I met a Catalan at Liverpool Central Station. Among all the things he said to me in the short while we were together the most curious is his sexual interpretation of English life. Sports in the open air? Sexuality. Flirting? Anything goes. Adultery? Just like anywhere else! Virginity? It does not matter at all. Homosexuality? Very widespread. And then, getting on to his train just as it was moving off, he turned and said to me, still standing on the platform:

'Women here make no bones about having a lover. What do you expect? English women don't have Latin *charme*!'

(Some time later, a close female friend of mine, commenting on the above passage, said to me: 'It's a statement of the obvious, as the works of Lawrence and Huxley clearly show.' I reminded her of something that Maurois had said: 'The England of Lawrence and Huxley does not exist.')

14 June

After two days in the English Lake District. – The mountains
of Cumbria, in the North-West of England, form a region
known by the name of The English Lake District or Lakeland.
The extremely high prestige of the area derives from a happy
combination of its natural beauty and associations with some
of the finest English poets and prose-writers of the nineteenth
century. The poetry emanating from its tranquil waters, its
tree-clad valleys and its imposing mountain tops has swollen
and become intensified from having been lovingly set down
in writing by men capable of expressing it, and from having
been the setting for large parts of their lives. The memory of
William Wordsworth, in particular, is so closely bound to this
part of the world that it has been given the fitting designation
of Wordsworthshire. He was born there and he died there, and
he spent there a large part of his life; in his poetry he sang of
all the places worthy of being celebrated in verse. In the small
cemetery around the church in Grasmere there is a simple
gravestone, no different from any of the others, which says
simply: William Wordsworth, 1850, Mary Wordsworth, 1859.

Reminders of the poet are in some degree found
everywhere. But in Grasmere and the surrounding area,
perhaps because he died and is buried there, they seem to be
sharper. He resided at Townend for eight years, in a small house
– Dove Cottage – converted now into a hallowed memorial
repository. At this time of the year the building disappears
almost completely amid the verdure of the surrounding trees,
the climbing roses and the Virginia creeper which completely encircle it. The house itself is tiny, like the garden, the

rooms having bare floorboards and very low ceilings. Through the small-paned windows there is a view, between the facing houses, of the leafy lakeside and then the mountains beyond. There is the library with its collection of editions of the poet's works and a set of portraits of him, the latter being dominated by the white-haired, pensive head of Wordsworth in old age; there is the room in which he used to sleep, containing his own bed with its canopy and heavy curtains; the kitchen in which the fire now burning seems not to have gone out since his time; a small side-chamber contains some timbers from the bed in which he died, at Rydal Mount, not far from Grasmere. Everything is carefully preserved, you are informed, with the greatest possible fidelity to how it all was in Wordsworth's days. And everywhere one detects a kind of fingerprint of his poetry, that poetry which delighted in proclaiming affection for all such humble things. The diary of his sister Dorothy makes this cosy setting even more familiar to us, because it allows us to reconstruct the life they led there. In the garden there still grow the kinds of plants mentioned by her in various entries, with the little flight of steps and the summerhouse which Wordsworth himself built and in which he composed some of his most glorious poems. In 1802, before leaving to be married and then to bring his new wife back to that place, he wrote that 'Farewell' which begins:

Farewell, thou little Nook of mountain-ground,
Thou rocky corner in the lowest stair
Of that magnificent temple…

Here in these same places we could evoke the memory of Samuel Taylor Coleridge, of his brother Hartley, of Robert Southey, of Thomas de Quincey, of John Wilson, and even of Shelley, who visited Keswick in 1812 and stayed for a time at Greta Hall.

It seems only natural that there should have been formed here The Lake School of Poetry. Travelling around this district one finds everywhere some marvellous places. Water, woodlands, mountains, flowers and dwellings are frequently arranged in perfect combination. On some occasions that perfection is such that it seems excessive, and so it is no longer perfection; in general, however, the harmony is total. The mountains, sometimes rough and jagged, often display shapely and solemn lines, and even though they do not reach great heights (the highest summit – Scafell Pike – does not make 1,000 metres), the sensation of being among big mountain summits never leaves you. Vegetation, where the fresh, bright green of oakwoods predominates, clothes many exquisite dales and the sides of ridges. Some of these mountain sides, though, are bare and rocky, with no other adornment than the strong-scented bracken, looking from afar like damp moss, which clings to the sides of distant peaks. Where the terrain is completely denuded whether on high or low ground – where flat expanses open up and dwellings become sparse, and also over the rough grazing land, when the rain falls tenaciously and one sees only sheep with shaggy fleeces, grazing quite indifferent to the downpour and to your passing through there – then the landscape takes on an almost tragic grandeur which chimes in with the local legends. One such tradition is represented in the pile of large stones which stands proud on the border of Cumberland and

Westmorland as a funeral monument to Dunmail, the last sovereign of Cumbria.

But this wildness in the countryside does not last for long. At a bend in the road or on reaching the top of a pass, one is suddenly surprised by the idyllic leafiness of a valley with its lake stretched out at one's feet. The waters' surface gleams like silver. The road takes you beneath thick, vast woodland like none that I can recall seeing anywhere except in England itself. Green meadows and fields, yellow or with a silvery hue, fill the expanses of the clearings. The houses, generally small, constructed from stone which the terrain provides (a kind of bluish-green slate, cut into flat blocks, built up in the dry-stone manner, with no mortar bonding, at least apparently so) pleasantly supply a human aspect to the landscape and complete the impression of peacefulness. Once again, and this time supremely, I have felt inside me the surge of a feeling that I have experienced on other occasions on my travels through England, a false reaction if you will, but no less moving even so: within those tranquil houses, whose interiors we glimpse through the little white curtains, must be the roosting place for happiness, only happiness, that sense of being at ease with the personal hand that life has dealt us, the greatest happiness to which we can aspire. Reality lies perhaps elsewhere, but I would be loath to renounce the belief that there is an element of truth in my appreciation. Something similar has been expressed, in more general terms, by the author of *La vie de Disraeli*, in an essay entitled 'As I see you'. These are the words of André Maurois: 'I think that you [the English] are the only truly happy people on this earth, because you do not expect too much from life… In general, mankind does not love happiness.

You do love it. And this is why you sometimes obtain it.'

Nowhere in England more than in the Lake District does the idea contained in these words seem to correspond so exactly to an objective fact.

18 June

Llangollen. – Among the most picturesque and best known places in North Wales the Vale of Llangollen figures prominently, with the River Dee skipping and babbling over the pebbles in its rocky bed, flowing between leafy bryns, and with the small town after which the Vale is called, stretched out on either side of the river and joined by a bridge of mellow brown stone, with its four pointed arches, which is known as one of the 'seven wonders of Wales'.

The word Llangollen – pronounced approximately 'chlangochlen' – means 'church of Saint Collen' and it is one of the innumerable Welsh place-names which begin with the word for church: Llanbedrog, Llanbelig, Llanbrynmair, Llandegai, Llandindrod, Llangammarch, etc., not forgetting the interminable name of the village to which Welshmen never fail to allude when speaking of the peculiarity of some of their place-names. Here is the full version, if the typesetter has, like me, enough patience to set it out in full:

Llanfairpwllgwyngyllgogerychwyrdrowllllantisiliogogogoch.
And it means, apparently:

Church – Mary – a hollow – white – walnut tree – near to – rapid – water-course – church of the Holy Name – red cave.

The village in question, however, which is none other than Llanfair, on the isle of Anglesey, is not to my knowledge ever designated with the full name but simply with the first two parts of it.

Let us return, though, to the Vale of Llangollen, entering it on the Ruabon side. Immediately after a coalmining and metal smelting area, we will find the unspoiled and pleasant valley. We can tour the streets of Llangollen, crowded with cheerful and chatty English housewives enjoying a daytrip from Chester or Crewe, from Shrewsbury or Wellington. Then a visit to the Gothic church and the cemetery surrounding it, without forgetting the funerary monument to the Ladies of Llangollen, two ladies of Irish stock who swore eternal friendship to one another, each preferring a life of celibacy to unwanted marriage, and who fled from their family homes in 1776, to live for half a century (until their deaths) in Llangollen. To our taste the church might seem too cold – a feeling we shall have in other Welsh churches – and, as we go about the streets, we shall feel some nostalgia for the gentle glow communicated by houses in the English Lake District. I would not go as far as to repeat, concerning Wales, what I wrote about the feeling of happiness which seemed to roost in those English cottages. Here we are in a country which is poorer and, probably, less attuned to the poetry of the 'hearth and home'.

Such reflections will not prevent us, however, from enjoying a delightful boat-trip on the Shropshire Union Canal. When I arrive at the landing-stage, the long narrow boat with a canopy over the seats is already full of English women. I am the only man to take a place on board. The merry wives laugh their heads off, they shout when speaking to one another, the conversation is peppered with snatches of song and slightly risqué allusions. One woman, toothless and with a prominent lower jaw, her bluish eyes bloodshot, straggly rust-coloured hair, her hat pushed right to the back of her head, begins to dance, stamping her feet on the deck and whooping into the damp, tranquil air of the late-afternoon. Another woman dips her hand into the murky stillness of the canal and brings out enough water to splash the performer's face. Were it not that I had earlier seen them coming out of a Temperance Hotel I should have believed that they had drunk rather to excess. The fulminating angry glare of a lady sitting close to them put an end to the scene.

Meanwhile the horse began to move. Horse? Yes: these narrow boats are towed by horses which go along at a fair speed on the path at the side of the canal, each with a smug young fellow mounted on its back. Whenever two barges cross in opposite directions, the horses are unhooked and the vessels continue to move, slowly, under the previous momentum. The same thing happens when a bridge must be gone under. And how extremely lovely it is to see the water and the greenness ahead, coming slowly closer, framed in the shape of the bridge's rough grey stone.

The canal glides along just above the valley bottom. Below where we are can be heard the sound of the river which feeds it, a river unlike the typical English ones, which tend to be narrow, with made up banks, slow running and deep. The memory of fast-flowing rivers in the Western Pyrenees comes suddenly and very vividly to mind on more than one occasion, and the countryside offers striking resemblances. Are we in Great Britain or in a valley of the Bearn or the High Navarre? Where does this path lead?

That last question does not come from me. I heard it later

from an old lady walking slowly all alone, detached from the noisy main throng, without an umbrella, in a torrential rainstorm, along the path between Chain Bridge and Llantysilio.

'If I am not mistaken,' I reply, making quick to give her shelter under my umbrella, 'It leads to Llantysilio church.'

'Are you Welsh?' she asks me after we have been walking along together in conversation.

I look at her in bemusement; but then I remember that in Wales there is a certain type of person, both male and female, who have a thoroughly South-European appearance. Popular wisdom attributes the phenomenon to the doings of Spaniards who survived the defeat of the Invincible Armada, many of them settling in Welsh territory.

When she made out the little church among the giant trees, by the river which ecstatically swells there in wide pools, my companion, whose prominent abdomen has been intriguing me, says to me in a slightly mysterious voice:

'I'm going to put on my hat to go into the church.'

And, without the slightest fuss, she tugs at the waistband of her skirt and pulls out a big hat all battered and misshapen.

'I put it in there so that it didn't get wet,' she adds as she is forcing the hat on to her head. And in the smile on her face I can make out, momentarily, a kind of reflection of the look that would have been in her eyes when she was a young woman.

The interior of the tiny church greatly belies its external aspect. Some flaking walls, some ancient wooden pews, some tombstones darkened with age would appeal more to our sensibility than this cold cleanliness of bright walls, shiny pews and lecterns and commemorative plaques of gilded metal. I have been informed that this coldness in Welsh places of worship is characteristic of the Methodism which prevails in the country and which aims to let nothing distract the worshipper's spirit from its communication with God.

As I emerge from Llantysilio church, rather disappointed but by no means put off, I set out under a fierce squall, almost cursing my archaeological whim, on the way which will take me to the ruins of the Cistercian abbey of Valle Crucis or, in Welsh, Mynachlog y Glyn, Minachlog Glyn Eliseg or Mynasog Pant y Groes, all of which names for the place are used by locals.

21 June

Manchester – The English are becoming seriously worried about the danger which, according to them, is threatening their country's rural landscape: the spread of urban and industrial development.

For those like me, who have not witnessed the preceding stages of occupation by these invaders armed with chimneys and entrenched in endless, uniform rows of brick houses, this concern does seem slightly exaggerated. There are sensitive English people who, like Mr. Baldwin only a few days ago, proclaim England to be the most beautiful country in the world, while knowing full well that in places where we are now struck by the aforementioned row upon row of roofs and chimneys there used to be until recently rolling fields scattered with enormous oaks, small cottages, tranquil sheep, superabundant cows, horses with mighty legs and long manes, fields through which there meandered a tranquil river twinned with a road. For such people the danger does really exist and something must be done to rescue from it, at least, some specially protected rural sites.

If there is anywhere in England where the invasion is particularly visible, it is in the fifty-kilometre stretch between Liverpool and Manchester. This does not mean that the rural landscape is not still holding out against the assault of industrialisation, but the process is insidiously taking over everywhere near and far, with white smoke or black smoke, with steam or the presence of a factory, of a metal or brick tall chimney. Every now and then it looks as if the peace of the fields will be fully restored, free from the menace; the last pall of smoke and the last spinning mill disappear with the horizon that the train leaves behind; but just as you have lost sight of them another army looms slowly and solemnly into view, confident of victory. On occasions this comes almost as a violent irruption, as when you reach Warrington, with its cotton and yarn mills, its iron-works and glass-works, with the blackness of its houses and the desolation of its streets, with the funereal turbidity of the water in its river and canal, overworked, long-suffering, blackish-green coloured, as expressive as some human faces. Warrington, as one passes through it, gives the impression of being one of the most horrible towns in England. Even so, I have been assured that it is one of the most prosperous.

Arrival in Manchester produces a similar impression of irruption, but now as something more coordinated and above all on a bigger scale, with a kind of orgy of scrap and rubble, coal, railway wagons, effluent, chimneys, storage hangars and smoke. Fog or rain binds everything into a unitary composition, giving to it a darker colour and making the scene more powerful. It must be remembered that Manchester is one of the cities with the highest rainfall in England. Liverpool people speak of it as being an uninhabitable place. And, in fact, it is not an unusual occurrence to depart from Liverpool in sunshine and arrive in a Manchester blanketed in fog. That is all there is to be said on the subject. Moreover, of the three great Northern industrial and mercantile cities, Liverpool has its River Mersey, wide and solemn, with a maritime look about it, with the docks lining its banks; Glasgow has the Clyde, with the prestige of its shipyards and of the picturesque river scenery; Manchester has only the filthy waters – if what one sees can be called water – of the Irwell, which zigzags between Manchester itself and Salford in an embanked, repugnant flow, hiding the shame of its ugliness behind houses and buildings. Looking down from one of the numerous bridges which cross it, I have thought more than once that it would perhaps be a good thing if this river were indeed channelled under ground: when all is said and done, the poor thing is nothing but a sewer.

The same can be said of the two small tributaries of the Irwell: the Medlock and the Irk. But it must be remembered, doing justice to these two pathetic 'rivers', that they feed the Manchester Ship Canal, a prodigious feat of engineering which has turned Manchester, an inland city, into one of the most bustling ports in Great Britain. When you get there you are surprised to see, almost in the heart of the city, vessels of very high tonnage. How the devil have they been able to steam into the industrial capital of England? They approached via the Crosby Channel, going up the Mersey, past Liverpool and Birkenhead, and then they sidled into the Manchester Ship

Canal, which is over fifty-six kilometres in length.

Manchester, as soon as you arrive there, gives an impression of strong and intense vitality which is not diminished at all as you go into the heart of the city. Thoroughfares like Market Street, Piccadilly, Deansgate or London Road have their own vigorous rhythm, a rhythm which is slowed down a little because of the vast number of people moving along them and because of the trams.

The impression of ugliness is not diminished here either. You can be temporarily distracted from it by the bright lights of the big stores, by the monumentality of certain buildings like the New Town Hall, the Assize Court, or by the elegance of others like the John Rylands Library. But the characterless side streets, the occasional view of one or other of Manchester's rivers, the sight of an unfortunate commemorative monument, like the one to Queen Victoria – badly served everywhere in this respect – delight in reminding you that all the aforementioned brilliance and grandeur are founded on monotony and ugly squalor. To be remarked upon, however, are two buildings that make one forget the oft-repeated reminders of Manchester's civic dreariness: the Rylands Library already mentioned, in its exquisite modern Gothic style, and Chetham College.

I have met English people who have visited Manchester often but who are unaware of the existence of this college. It is nonetheless one of the sites most worthy of visiting there. It stands close to the cathedral – itself very insignificant – and by the side of the monastic-looking Grammar School. But do not expect to find a tranquil, ancient place. Life buzzes all around there: Exchange Station, Victoria Station, the Exchange building where the cotton trading is done, are all very close by. But the spacious yard where the pupils play (Chetham College is for orphan boys) seems to set it apart from the bustle and the day-to-day. And when you have knocked at the library entrance and have climbed up the dark, narrow staircase which leads to it, once you are inside there, you have the feeling of having slipped, suddenly but gently, back into the silence of centuries gone by. Tightly packed black wooden book-stacks which form corridors and reading spaces; windows which supply a considerate half-light and which make you think what this library must be like during the winter fogs; and, coming from the books, the wooden shelves and reading desks, an aroma of antiquity and of learning, an aroma reminiscent of Oxford.

And the impression of contrast – perhaps rather, of confluence – between the modern and the ancient Manchester, something we have been unable to find anywhere as strong as here, never leaves you for a moment when you are visiting the buildings and the rooms of Chetham College. You encounter it in the reading room, decorated with portraits of illustrious Mancunians, in the dining hall with its traditional tables and benches, in the dormitory, where innumerable children's beds face smilingly up towards the high, blackened roof-timbers; you see it when you look at the pupils wearing a uniform which has not changed since the days of the founder Humphrey Chetham (1653), as well as when you look at their bathing pool and the workshop where they begin the study of skilled trades.

When you leave that place you are submerged once more in the noisy traffic and bustle. But you are sharply aware that you have just added an essential feature, quite distinct from all the others, to the image of Manchester which will always stay with you.

*

Returning from Manchester: – In my compartment, directly in front of me, a man who appears to be drunk: beneath his red hair, thick and combed back, in the flushed, coarse feature of his face, two pale eyes gaze out with a strange shine. He looks filthy. He has a flower in his lapel, and he is calmly eating cake and bananas. Suddenly he speaks to me. What does he say? Heavens above! He tells me that I am very intelligent. And the better to make me understand him, he points at his forehead, he runs a hand over his hair to smooth it down backwards, and then, making arm movements as though he were playing an invisible violin, makes a shrill, grating noise... Then he becomes silent again and falls asleep. From time to time a shudder makes his body jerk.

22 June

Southport. – At Preston into our carriage came a middle-aged man, rather stocky, with prematurely grey hair. Conversation began with a remark on the invariable lateness of that particular train's departure, the last one of the day for Liverpool; then there was the usual question – 'Which country are you from?' – followed now by the most unexpected enquiry: 'Where did you have that suit made?' To which he added, 'Don't be surprised at the question. I am a tailor, in Southport.'

Southport is one of six places designated as 'famous holiday resorts' of the North of England. The other five are: Blackpool, Harrogate, Buxton, Llandudno and Scarborough. Famous seaside resorts or spas, they each have their numerous, sparkling clientele of English and American visitors. And, although the season is only just beginning, I did not want to leave England without having visited at least one of these places. Southport and Llandudno were the ones chosen, on account of their relative proximity to Liverpool. This is what prompted me to get the man I was talking with on the train to tell me something about his town, having heard him say 'I am a tailor, in Southport'.

He did so with more enthusiasm than eloquence, but not without exciting my interest. He praised the wide streets, the modern buildings, the fresh green of abundant trees, the luxury department stores. In particular he spoke highly of the opportunities for bathing, especially the new sea-bathing lake. And of these places what he waxed most lyrical about was, above all, the beauty of the female bathers. A kind of dream-like sweetness gleamed in his eyes as he talked about the delightful young ladies, the 'lovely girls', of Southport's bathing facilities.

I thought it would be appropriate for me to say some complimentary things – sincerely complimentary, I can add – about the physical attractiveness of English women. 'Well, if that is what you like,' said the discerning tailor, 'you really must go to Southport. There you will see some striking beauties.' And with his fingertips he drew two imaginary curves, one in each direction, over his chest, in a swift gesture that was more eloquent than all his laudatory words.

I did go to Southport. And I admired everything that my travelling companion extolled. I cannot tell what sort of impression this town might give at a different time of year, without the abundance of trees and plants which now dominates its streets and gardens. In winter things will be different, with mists and with a sea which even in good weather looks uninviting and somewhat cheerless. Today, though, in the sunshine and with a refreshing stiff breeze, even though it is a workday, it felt like a town on holiday, brisk and jolly.

I went to see where people bathe: a wide, open-air swimming pool, with some shelter provided by the public viewing gallery (where for three or four pence, depending on the time of day, you can enjoy a pleasing spectacle), a Greco-Roman temple – the cafeteria – presiding over the separate facilities for bathers, males on one side of the pool and females on the other. One only has to see where all the spectators are gathered in order to work out which side is reserved for women. Then something else will be observed, which is that all of them, attractive or not, young or old, are wearing a swimsuit – or at least the knitted two-piece version which, with its skimpy bottom, is just as revealing. I enquired whether the knitted swimming costume had been so absolutely the norm for a long time. And I was amazed to learn that girls of seventeen or eighteen could not remember anything other being worn for bathing.

This fact gives considerable food for thought. The phenomenon in question occurs in bashful Albion, quite publicly and since who knows when. In other countries, even young and extremely modern-minded ones, the swimsuit has given rise to protests and strong reactions. And what we see in this is one more distorted view on the part of the moralisers. In order to cleanse away completely the unhealthy, sinful mystery surrounding the human body – a distortion often attributable to the moralisers themselves – there is nothing better than the triple alliance of fresh air, water and light.

The strongly, constantly flowing cascades shine blue; the breeze ruffles the surface of the pool. Bodies glisten, tanned or pale, dripping water, basking in sunshine and youthfulness. Brightly coloured swimsuits catch the light. Feminine exclamations, like cheery bugle notes – *lovely!*, *splendid!* – punctuate the diving, the swift descents on the water-slide, the chasing round the pool-side. A blue swimsuit dashes by, then a green one, then a white one. A satyr lifts up a pink swimsuit and carries her into the water, eventually depositing her, with a vigorous heave, on the central floating island where a sort of pot-bellied Bacchus, surrounded by youthful nymphs, is attempting a balancing act. Some attractive young women lie indolently on the lawn which encircles with green the poolside asphalt. They have made sure to have with them their cigarettes, and their make-up purses with mirror, face-powder and lipstick. Their swim-caps have been worn only for as long as they were in the water, which enables them then to show off the marvellous golden sheen of their hair when they shake it out. Whoever dared to say that short hair is not pretty? A little way off another beauty – an odd exception – with a fine display of long hair. Just compare the two and then tell me if short hair does not win the day, aesthetically.

Once again the swim-suited runners dash noisily by. Now they are playing leapfrog. The spectators look on benignly and laugh at their frolics. The sky clears to show pale blue patches among white clouds. We have a view over the town, with its parade of hotels and well-to-do residences, and it now assumes a serious air. Some familiar notes come from the band. Is it not the Song to the Evening Star from *Tannhäuser*? It does sound rather like it. But, in this setting, at this time of day and, especially, with this rhythm? Wolfram singing to the enchanting star with a Charleston accompaniment! Have we not got it wrong? No, no: it is *Tannhäuser* for sure. Here are the pilgrims returning from Rome, having no doubt got lost along the way. Their solemn chanting… their solemn chanting has a jaunty two-step rhythm. What do you expect? They are pilgrims who know how to adjust to their circumstances. But we are hurriedly getting ready to leave. We are unsettled by the thought that, if we stay just a short while longer, we shall perhaps see them emerging from the changing cabins, no longer clad in their smocks and with their pilgrims' crooks, but in the latest American-style swimsuit.

23 June

On the way to Llandudno. Zinc on one side – the sea – sapphire green on the other – fields. Gulls, gulls, gulls everywhere, all the way to infinity.

Conway. A bay, a small town, a large castle. Too much of a castle – like others on this island (Dover Castle, the Tower of London itself) – to the extent that there is something pastiche or toy-like about it, not to do with its size but with the appearance of its fabric – cardboard – and its outline – stylised.

Llandudno. A town with wide streets, full of hotels and boarding houses. A marvellous sea-front promenade. An almost circular bay with a tower at each end. Combinations of colours: matt green, stark rock (greyish), red hues of houses and roofs.

The beach is pebbly, with few people on it, despite the pleasant sunshine. Nothing elegant catches the eye. The

Americans have not yet arrived. One of the very few female bathers, a youngish woman, wears a hired costume which fits her too loosely, and her flaccid breasts, bluish with the cold, look pathetic. Her friend is signalling to her, with gestures the swimmer cannot understand, to hitch up her costume. The scene – shortly to be repeated – is so pitiful that nobody laughs, or even smiles.

Some enormous motor buses go by – blue, yellow, red – packed with people out to enjoy the weekend.

Saturday evening draws in, as dismal as if it were a Sunday evening.

24 June

Although I had crossed the Wirral Peninsula from West Kirby to Birkenhead so many times, were it not for this afternoon's trip I would have retained a completely false impression: just the wintry impression of a vast and desolate place.

Now, instead, having travelled by bus rather than by train, I shall retain the memory of a beautiful countryside, a kind of spring-time garden of delights full of ineffable surprises, bathed in the warm exuberant afternoon sunshine. Everywhere there was a gladness, a sense of well-being and of calm. Cottages and small houses reflected the light back, neat and clean. The red clay of the tennis courts harmonised sweetly with the whiteness of the line-markings and of the players' clothes, with the dense greenness of the vegetation. The sunlight played, sliding in and out, spurting between all the different shades of green.

25 June

Taking leave of Liverpool. – Before leaving for England, more specifically for Liverpool, I attempted quite naturally to obtain some information about the place. 'Liverpool is horrible at every time of year,' wrote a friend who had resided there for long periods. 'Oh, most certainly not!' was the brusque reaction of an important person in whose presence I was reporting that judgement. 'I have been there: in Liverpool there is much to admire, things that take your breath away.' When I returned from the first of my two years there, I was asked by a fragile, other-worldly scholar, smiling as though he were talking about a tiny idyllic borough, 'So, Liverpool is as pretty as ever, then?'

These are three opinions which it is difficult to reconcile and which demonstrate to what extent human beings can have different views on the same thing. Now, with two academic years in Liverpool behind me, about to take definitive leave of the place, I can easily understand my friend's harsh judgement, our important person's opinion seems admissible to me, and I can still be impressed by the private rapture of our scholar.

The friend in question lived for a long time in Liverpool, working there and having to put up with the climate. He saw the city on days when the weather was fine, when the River Mersey gleams with happiness and the ships which cleave its waters seem to be at play there, and when along the bustling streets there is that kind of joyfulness which a bright sunny day transmits to people at large in countries with inclement climates. But he also saw the place, much more frequently, with its streets all sad, rain pouring down, or in that typical fog which rises up, there in the middle of the very street, like a weary cloud of dust. Nor was his a restricted view of Liverpool: he did not limit himself to going up and down only the streets which form the heart of the city, from the port to St. George's Hall, from Exchange Station to the Custom House, streets where one finds merchant bankers' and shipping companies' offices, travel agencies and luxury department stores, restaurants and dance-halls. Nor did he limit himself to the tree-lined, spacious suburbs in the vicinity of Princes Park and Sefton Park. His business, or his curiosity, must have taken him into more crowded and poverty-stricken districts, particularly as opulence and hardship are such close neighbours in Liverpool that they are separated by only a few short steps. Thus, close to the luxury of the Midland Adelphi Hotel and Lewis' department store is the bottom of Brownlow Hill with its squat and sordid houses, with its second-hand shops where grey-bearded Jews in bowler hats pile high their motley stock in eye-catching display, with the strong smell coming from fried-fish shops, with the drifting music of an organ-grinder, an infinitely melancholy sound even in places where the atmosphere is most edgy and threatening. And across the whole of this side of the city out to Wavertree, or in the Welsh district of Everton and so many other parts, there are so many streets which look just the same or even worse. Row after dirty row of houses whose brickwork is smoke-blackened, each one with four or five steps outside leading up to the door, with a basement where the tenants cook and eat, where the table is always laid and where the light is often on even in broad daylight. Horrible streets, where barefooted children play, their clothing all ragged and patched, their faces like those of criminals. Sometimes, on foggy days, going along one of those streets or crossing a junction, looking at that scenario of grim urban desolation so much worse than any desolate natural landscape, I have wondered: 'But, what is this? Can it really be?' It looks like a kind of hell, chill and slimy, designed to punish sybarites from cities that are soft and warm, caressed by sunlight, by a gentle sea and by the firmament.

There is another, quite different Liverpool: the one which must have been seen by the important person I referred to earlier. He must have gone there towards the end of spring or during the summer; and he must have been captivated by the neo-classical buildings, libraries and museums, standing side by side, and even more enchanted by St. George's Hall, a magnificent Greco-Roman edifice which is one of the best proofs there are of how tasteful and skilled were English architects of the 19th century in adapting styles from the past. And it also makes us think regretfully about the state of our own Palace of Music.[33] He will have visited Princes Park and Sefton Park, in the sunshine, with the sound of birds singing and the sight of courting couples. He would have walked along the busy streets near to the Landing Stage (Church Street, Lord Street, Castle Street) and been able to become absorbed in the rhythm of central Liverpool's bustle. A lively and quick-moving throng, predominantly female, fills the pavements with bodies and their chatter. In these streets, at one o'clock or at

33   The Palau de la Música Catalana in Barcelona was designed by the architect Lluís Domènech i Muntaner (1850–1923), a contemporary of Antoni Gaudí (1852–1926). Cons-tructed 1905–08, it is one of the finest and most emblematic buildings from the phase of Catalan *Modernisme*. Soldevila's remark here reflects changes in architectural fashion that he himself had witnessed, against *modernista* exuberance and favouring classical or rationalist styles. Since the latter half of the twentieth century the Palau de la Música has enjoyed its recovered status as an architectural masterpiece.

three o'clock in the afternoon, you are aware without any need for statistical evidence that the feminine population is in the majority in England. Nowadays, with the fashion for short skirts (and in Liverpool they are shorter for sure than virtually anywhere else in Europe) the sense of this demographic imbalance seems to be multiplied. Before lunch time the movement of female legs, in Lords Street or Church Street, is so intense that it makes one's head spin.

Our important person must have visited Liverpool years ago and he would have been spared that curious sensation. He would have gone peacefully along his way to the Landing Stage, to contemplate from there the wide rippling expanse of the Mersey at the port, which is in my view the finest thing that the city has to offer. Whether in the depths of winter, when the waters are the colour of zinc and the horizons are dark with fog or smoke, through which one can just make out the tightly packed urban shapes on the other bank; or in clear weather, when the waters now look almost blue, and the horizons take on a golden shine, the Mersey has a powerful beauty. And at any time of the year, among the finest spectacles that one can enjoy is either a ferry trip to Birkenhead, Wallasey, New Brighton or Rock Ferry, Wirral towns on the Cheshire side, or else a ride on the Overhead Railway.

This electric train glides along the length of the docks, at roof height. The wharves line the banks of the river, for nearly seven miles. This is not a spatially concentrated port like ours in Barcelona; here is a single great port which has been unravelled into a succession of other ones. The effect is surprising. Here are docks which are among the largest in the world, with powerful pumping systems to fill them quickly (the Canada Graving Dock, 240 metres in length, can be filled in an hour and a half) and super-efficient unloading and transport machinery. The still, greenish water contained in the basin holds aloft the impressive architecture of ocean liners belonging to White Star, Cunard, Leyland and the other vast navigation companies. Enormous cranes stand out against the sky in tragic postures. Some dry docks have vessels in them for repair, with their anchors and chains hanging from the sides all twisted together like some great snakes at rest.

Certainly: in Liverpool there are many things to admire. I can understand the admiration of that important person I have just mentioned. But how are we to understand the scholar in his vague rapture? 'Liverpool as pretty as ever?' said with a smile like that of someone evoking an angelic vision. How, when and in what mood must he have seen the place? If his nature were not as it was, I should believe that he had seen it through the eyes of one of those young Lancashire women, who are renowned for being so pretty.

27 June

The examinations were held yesterday. I leave this evening. I have seen it through to the end. There were times, during the months of January and February, when I thought that it would be impossible. This period in my life is now closed.

> *Anges revêtus d'or, de pourpre et d'hyacinthe,*
> *O vous, soyez témoins que j'ai fait mon devoir.*[34]

34   'Angels dressed in gold, in purple, and in hyacinth blue,/ O you, be witnesses that I have done my duty.'

Appendix[35]

Palautordera,[36] June 1928

O*n the subject of trust.* When you arrived in England three years ago you formed an impression that the English were mistrustful of foreigners. Going through the station buildings in Dover – supposing that you had travelled this way – you were surprised by two signs which divided the passengers who had just left the train: 'British Citizens, Foreigners'. At no other border had you ever encountered such a distinction between citizens and foreigners, and you were certainly surprised by it then, naturally. Some people took it as a kind of offence and they muttered some rather angry indignation or made some humorous comments.

35   The pages below contain journal entries made by Soldevila very soon after leaving England. They were incorporated by Enric Pujol in his 2011 edition of *Hores angleses* (Adesiara, Barcelona), their content relating directly to the Liverpool experience as originally published - albeit without the original freshness and agility. Our incorporation here of this more stiffly formal material does serve, however, to set in relief the spontaneity and variety of the main text as it originally appeared.

36   The author was very attached to Santa Maria de Palautordera, close to the picturesque massif of the Montseny mountain (Vallès Oriental district), where the Soldevila family had a summer residence.

This distinction has lately disappeared. The formalities are carried out during the Channel crossing: showing the visa stamped in your passport, handing over the form that you had to fill in, undergoing questioning about your journey. This sort of interrogation is also, as a general rule, peculiar to entry into England. Only exceptionally does it happen in other countries of Western Europe. You are asked what you are going to do in England, how long you plan to stay, if you have ever been there before, etc. Then sometimes they consult a book whose purpose and function I have never understood.

Once you have had the interview with the Registration Officer, it is as though your condition had changed. Your very first contact with the English is marked by a feeling of being mistrusted, but from that moment on you will frequently come across situations which demonstrate that English life is built upon foundations of mutual trust.

As soon as the ship has docked and been invaded by the porters and the landing-crew, scuttling down the gangway like monkeys, you will have the strong sensation that you have entered a different world as far as this matter of trust is concerned. You point out your hand luggage to a porter: without hardly stopping he makes a mental note of which are the bags in question; pointing at them he tells you the number with which they have been labelled; he gives you a card with this number on it; he tells you that you can now go to the customs office and he will meet you there; and off he goes, as quickly as he had arrived, without picking up your luggage. You will hesitate for a while before leaving your possessions among that great crowd of people. But finally, you will make up your mind; if you call a different porter and ask about it, when he sees you have your card with the number on it he will tell you to go straight to customs. And sure enough: your porter will be there; or if he is not there yet, he will not be long in turning up.

Upon arrival in London you will straightway be presented with another demonstration of trust. You yourselves will show the porter which trunks are yours: you will open them in the presence of the customs officer (in Dover only your hand luggage has been checked), they will be put into a taxi for you and only as you are leaving the station precinct (the taxi rank is inside, adjoining the platforms) will a policeman ask if your luggage is as listed on your booking schedule. This regulated control applies only to travellers arriving from the Continent with forms on which their baggage is declared. If your journey continues beyond the capital you will observe that the checking-in method has been greatly simplified: and this simplification operates on a sound basis of trust, trust in the people who handle the luggage and trust in the travellers themselves. No paperwork of any kind. The porter who has taken charge of your trunks and bags, at the station from which you are departing, puts a destination label on each item, weighing those which he thinks might exceed the weight-limit, takes them to the luggage-van, pointing out where they are being stored, and that is the end of the story. Once at your destination, you go personally to collect your luggage, indicating which are your trunks or suitcases, and these are then handed to you without more ado.

This first impression you get during your journey coming into England is progressively reinforced in the next few days. The day after my first arrival in London I went to the Westminster

Bank to cash a cheque. It was not an exorbitant amount but it was not insignificant either, especially for me. I was astounded: they paid me without even asking to see my passport! I remembered the troubles that a foreigner has in our country. Later, in the dealings I had with banks (in England there is no way to live without dealing with banks) I often had occasion to marvel, and sometimes to worry, about the way they did things: only on the basis of unconditional good faith and of perfectly accurate accounting can one understand the way in which these matters are handled in England.

Here are some instances.

Current accounts are recorded in a passbook, a kind of document where, as with our bank books, payments in and withdrawals are registered.[37] But, unlike in our banks, the entry in the passbook is not recorded immediately (unless you can make a strong case for having this done) but the day after taking it to the bank. So you make a deposit into your account without receiving any proof at all of having done so. They do fill out a printed receipt for the sum deposited. This, however, is a document signed by you but retained by them.

One day I told an English friend of my surprise about this way of doing things. He explained to me how he made his deposits, seemingly pleased to be able to explain to me a procedure which, to his eyes, was thoroughly satisfactory. His explanation, however, left me even more fascinated. 'I post to them,' he said, 'the passbook and the amount I want to pay in; next day the passbook is sent back with the sum duly recorded there.' So his procedure demonstrated another kind of trust:

---

37   Subsequently the passbook was replaced by single-transaction forms which are easier to send by post.

trust in the postal service.

Here is another example:

I wanted to move my current account from the Liverpool branch to the one in Birkenhead. In Liverpool I was told to make out a cheque, and that they would then fill in the amount by which my account was in credit. So I signed a blank cheque. If there were to have been a mistake (without any allowing for any devious impropriety) they would have been able to show my signature confirming the certified amount I had withdrawn from the Liverpool branch to pay into the Birkenhead one.

Lastly, so as not to protract these reminiscences on the subject of banking, in West Kirby, a small town where I lived for some months, I once went to my local branch to deposit an amount in pesetas. The sterling equivalent had to be calculated. They did not know the exchange rate for that day. They had to consult Liverpool. Instead of doing this immediately by telephone, they told me that the deposit would be credited the following day. They held on to my pesetas without giving me any kind of receipt.

Every time I faced a situation like the ones mentioned I left the bank partly bemused and partly worried. But seeing that everything worked smoothly and with scrupulous exactness, I finally became accustomed to it.

And now for some examples of a different kind.

From my earliest days in the University of Liverpool I kept noticing how, propped against the walls of corridors and staircases, there were always some bags or satchels (of a sort not very different from those carried by students in our country) which are used by a lot of people in England, men as well as women, to carry not only their books, diaries, papers, but also the most diverse bits of equipment. I recall that on one occasion, on the tram, a satchel of that kind suddenly fell open, to the great though silent disquiet of all the passengers and to the great embarrassment of the girl to whom it belonged. Among the items which fell out if it there was a delicate and fetching blue silk chemise. I had bent down impetuously to lend a hand and so it fell to me to return the garment solicitously to her. In performing this service I was reminded of the origin and the motto of the Order of the Garter, while she was turning red with acute embarrassment: *Honi soit qui mal y pense.*

The owners of bags like that particular one used to leave them lying around in the University corridors. The Administration was obliged to put up signs, visible for a few days, requesting an end to the practice. 'Has anything wrong happened?' I asked, referring discreetly to possible theft. 'No, but it might,' was the reply.

The specialised library collections are located on the University site itself. There is no supervision and students have free access to the books, not only to read on the premises but also to take them home. The same is true of the main library, with the difference that there are librarians here: their job is not to keep an eye on you, however, but to provide you with the titles which are not on open access.

The fact is that where English trustfulness was brought home to me in a most striking way was in a hotel in Keswick, in the Lake District. It was a very charming hotel, in a fine setting. Once inside my room I wanted, naturally, to lock it: there was no key in the lock, and there was neither a bolt nor a latch, nor any other way of shutting fast the door.

'You have forgotten to give me the key,' I said to the maid, thinking it was a perfectly natural comment to make.

'Key? Oh, no, there isn't a key.'

'There are one or two rooms with lock and key,' chimed in another maid whose curiosity had drawn her towards where we were, 'but very few indeed.'

'How can the door be securely closed, then?'

'Oh, there's no need: in this hotel, there is nothing to worry about!'

Palautordera, August 1928

Use of the postal service. – Only a few days after embarking on my life in England, I lost an umbrella – an event which frequently blights my existence. I had mislaid it, I thought, on a journey which I was beginning to become used to making: Birkenhead Park to Liverpool Central. I enquired at the lost property office in the latter station. It had not been handed in.

'It must be at Birkenhead Central,' they told me.

I mentioned the matter to a colleague at the University.

'I'll now have to go to Birkenhead Central,' I said.

'No: why should you?' he retorted quickly. 'Just write to them.'

'Write?' I said, not a little taken aback.

'Obviously. What was your umbrella like?' And without waiting for my answer he took out his fountain pen and began drafting the letter: 'Yesterday, between B'head Park and L'pool Central, I think I mislaid an umbrella which was this colour, that size, and so on… I shall be grateful if you can tell me whether it has been handed in at B'head Central.'

The next day I had a reply on a standard card – evidence that this was a normal situation and procedure. My 'lost umbrella' had not been handed in. I had been saved a wasted journey.

'In Spain,' a colleague told me when we were commenting on the matter, 'the postal service is not used like it is here… And what is worse,' he added with a smile, 'is that letters are usually not answered.' And he went on: 'Not long ago, there was at the University of X a Spanish lecturer to whom I had to write for professional reasons. No response came from him. I wrote to him again, after a while, expressing mild surprise. Then I did receive a brief reply: he averred that he had never received my original letter. 'I shall appreciate it' – my colleague insisted – 'if you can find out what happened to that letter, because a letter should not get lost. And as I can recall perfectly the date, time and place of posting, if it does not turn up, I shall address an appropriate enquiry to the postmaster there.' It was not long before the letter was discovered inside an old cupboard where it had been placed – according to the Spanish lecturer – during one of his absences.

This story seemed very typical to me. Combined with the episode of the lost umbrella, it constituted my initiation into this aspect of English life. It seemed to me, however, that my colleague's veiled threat was quite empty and that he had made it simply to frighten his indolent correspondent. 'Can it really be true,' I asked myself, 'even if the place, the day and the time of posting are known, that a letter can go missing for days and still be found?' One day my own mail contained part of the address wrapper of a newspaper to which I subscribed. The wrapper, with my address on it, was stuck on to a printed form. This form read as follows: 'The item from which the attached wrapper has become detached cannot at present be identified.

It may have been delivered to you separately or returned to the sender. If you have not received it and you know that it has not been returned, further searches will be carried out, if that is your wish, provided that this form is duly completed and sent, together with the address label, to The Controller, London, etc. If further investigation is not required, this form should be destroyed.' There were five sections to be filled in. One of these was headed 'place, date and time of posting'. Clearly, then, my colleague's threat was based on a foundation in reality.

I had no interest in further searches being carried out, but I did not follow the advice about destroying the official form. Since I come from a country where the postal service attaches so little importance to printed matter, that scrap of address wrapper, so carefully rescued and attached to that form, possessed a symbolic value. I have kept it ever since.

It must be said, though, that if an organisation like the British Post Office shows consideration taken to such an extreme, this also demonstrates that it may not be unusual for wrappers or labels to become detached while under the responsibility of that service. The sea is to blame. To avoid the effects of storms in the English Channel, the administrations of certain continental newspapers use stronger wrapping on copies sent to England. Our own newspapers should follow this example. The wrappers of *La Publicitat* and *La Nau* are often torn when they arrive; *La Veu* uses slightly stronger ones.[38] The force of the storms must sometimes be so great that even the stronger wrapping is damaged: I have kept one

38   *La Publicitat* (see note 1 on page 19); *La Nau*, short-lived (1927–23) Catalan-language daily of liberal-democratic nationalist affiliation. *La Veu de Catalunya* (1899–1937) was the widely influential organ of conservative Catalan nationalism and its 'establishment' before the Civil War.

address-strip of the *Journal de Genève* which arrived with no paper inside.

And since we are discussing how our press stands up to being shipped to England, it would perhaps be worth mentioning that journals do not usually have sufficient postage paid on them. A large-format illustrated magazine was sent to me with just a two-cent stamp strangely folded, almost invisible, over the edge of the big envelope. In England items with underpaid postage are charged twice the amount owing, and so I ended up paying seven and a half pence (around 80 Spanish cents) as 'postage due'.

Even so, this is preferable to the procedure followed in such cases by the Spanish mail service within 'national territory'. It is very familiar to my readers: the letter or item in question is retained in the despatching office: if the sender can be identified he receives notification of this; if not, the notification goes to the addressee for him to send the missing stamps to the place of posting. Outcome: a delay of several days in delivery of the letter, and the risk, or actual consequences, of damage done by the effects of the hold-up.

As I was settling into life in England, I came increasingly to understand the extraordinary use made there of postal correspondence. Extraordinary, that is, compared with normal use in our part of the world: normal, however, if one takes into account the innumerable advantages to be derived from intelligently making use of the service. Situations like those that arise in our country would be inconceivable. A few days ago I received a letter from a man telling me that he needed to see me over a matter that was important to me. I had to make a special trip to Barcelona. When we came face to face he told me that a particular form was needed for him to complete the commission he was handling for me. 'Heavens above!' I exclaimed. 'Could you not have explained that in your original letter, instead of making me travel here just so that I could hear it from your lips!' Similar situations abound, and everybody must have experienced something like it, either as a protagonist or as a victim.

'England is a country where lots of letters are written, perhaps because it is one of the very few places where it is usual for them to be replied to,' wrote Salvador de Madariaga in the 'London sketches' he published in his book *Quatre espagnols à Londres*.[39] But use of the post there is usual not only for letters: all kinds of packages are delivered to the door. This is not exclusive to England, but England is certainly one of the countries where the service, so underused in our society, is most fully utilised.

Finally, to give an idea of the extent to which relations there are conducted by post, we can say that all academic affairs are managed through written communication. Items of business, even the most minor ones, will never be dealt with by word of mouth, except, I think, in certain exceptional cases, as when a face-to-face reprimand or warning might have to be given.

An example that says it all: one morning, towards the end of the first term, when I was expecting to be called in order to be handed the first quarter of my annual salary, I received

39   Madariaga (1886–1978) held posts in the secretariat of the League of Nations from 1921 to 1928, before moving to the Chair of Spanish in Oxford (1928–31). Subsequently he was a diplomat and then government minister during the Spanish Republic. He went into exile in England with the advent of the Franco regime, becoming a prominent figure in international liberalism and in the project for a united Europe. *Quatre espagnols à Londres* was published in Paris in 1928. *His Englishmen, Frenchmen, Spaniards. An Essay in Comparative Psychology* (Oxford University Press, 1929) is close in spirit to Soldevila's perspective.

through the post an official envelope from the University. Inside I found a cheque. Nothing else: I had been paid.

I thought back to the Spanish payroll system and the endless lists which have to be drawn up, sent to Madrid and then back to the local Treasury office, signed by each individual when payment is made, and then sent back to Madrid. Of course, the complexity of all this entails another complicating factor in order for the procedure to work at all well: the services of the bursar whose job it is to deal with all those details and whose salary is related to the size of the payroll.

On comparing expeditious English simplicity with the cumbersome Hispanic complexity, we observe the contrasting use made of the postal service: the former to make things easier, the latter to make life harder.

Palautordera, September 1928

Correspondence with the Inland Revenue. – Discussing the subject of postal services in England, I left on one side a topic which well deserves its own separate chapter. This subject acquires an immediate relevance, as the time of year comes round once again for us all to renew our personal documentation. Everybody complains about the hours they have to waste, about the queuing that has to be done in order to obtain that tiny, and expensive, bit of paper. And to think that it could all be made so much easier! Why can it not be done through the post? That is how these things are done in England; not, of course, in order to get one´s identity card, something which they do not have, but in order to pay income tax.

I had come back to Barcelona to spend the Christmas

holidays when, one morning, I received an oblong envelope whose function, declared in large black letters, was: On His Majesty's Service.

I opened it with some trepidation, thinking what the devil could they want from me on His British Majesty's Service? All they required was completion of a printed form (a 'tax return'), giving my employment, my salary and other income, my marital status, number of children, etc., not very different, really, from our *empadronament* or electoral registration form. I did very carefully what was required, after having conscientiously read the instructions supplied with the form. At the very most, I spent no more than a quarter of an hour on it. The form was on its way back to England a few days before I left for the same destination.

Upon arriving home, I found another envelope, a smaller one this time, which similarly displayed the pompous words 'On His Majesty's Service'. It contained the request for the favour of a prompt reply to the previous communication from the Inspector of Taxes. A change of address together with my journey to Barcelona and back had delayed the arrival of my reply, and they were now prompting me to respond immediately. I wrote a couple of lines saying that the form had been returned on such and such date from Barcelona; and I had a quick look at the information provided, 'penalties' section. The first paragraph said:

'Failure to submit a return, or a false or incorrect declaration will incur a fixed penalty of 20 pounds sterling, plus triple the amount of the tax due. A penalty of no more than 5 pounds sterling can be imposed for non-submission of a return, even if the person named can show that he was not liable for tax.'

If I had omitted to send back the completed form, I could have expected a fine of 5 pounds maximum, but I had done what was required of me, and had no cause for concern. My return was probably already with Mr. Tax Inspector by then.

In fact, a few days later I received a brief letter from him – just five lines. I had declared only half of my university salary, as I took up my post in October, which meant that only my emoluments from October to April would be taxable in that financial year. In the tax office they understood that perfectly well, but they assured me they would be very pleased if I would like to let them know all the details of my employment since April 6 last. I obliged, and I heard nothing further from them for the rest of that year. £135 per year (approximately 4,000 pesetas) is the personal allowance, the amount considered necessary for a single man to live comfortably and simply in England, and this amount is untouchable, non-taxable. For the married man living with his wife (which is my case), the tax-free allowance is raised to £225: half of my university salary did not amount to that. This meant that the Great British treasury received no contribution from me, and so I did not yet get to know from personal experience how the eventual collection of income tax worked.

I did find this out in the following financial year. I was caught between two tax cycles but my full annual remuneration would naturally have to be declared in the end. Just in case I had any doubts about this, a note from the University finance department notified me: 'The following amounts will be declared in relation to payments made to you by the University...' When things are so carefully organised, always by post, it is almost impossible for mistakes to occur. Needless to say, it is not advisable to try it on deliberately. *Penalties*: 'The penalty for fraudulent evasion or untrue declaration of information when claiming allowances or reductions is fixed at £20 plus three times the tax due on all income sources. Anyone deliberately making an untrue declaration or representation in order to obtain any allowance, deduction, discount or refund against income tax payments, either in their own name or through another agency, or in any submission relating to income tax, will be summarily sentenced to not more than six months' imprisonment with hard labour.'

Six months of hard labour! The English do not take these matters lightly, and I doubt that any Englishman would risk any kind of concealment to reduce his tax bill. Can you just imagine what would happen on Hispanic soil, if all those who make false declarations were to be condemned to hard labour? What battalions of them there would be!

A few months later, at the end of March, I received the Notice of Assessment informing me of the amount due from me in tax: I had twenty-one days in which to make any formal appeal. I found everything correct and fair, and I lodged no objection. Finally, dated the end of June, I received a last form which stated again, now firmly and without any possible appeal, the amount due and my duty to pay it within ten days. Was it now finally time to show up at an office and, with no more to it, make the actual payment? Out of the question: I could pay in cash if I wanted to, but I could do it also by cheque or by postal order. I used the latter procedure – without charge, as is any mail use related to the income tax. The next day I had the appropriate receipt in my hands: the postman had brought it.

This straightforward procedure, which saves time, uncertainty and mistakes – even simpler than it seems in the explanation I have just given – would it be workable in this country or not?

Many readers will possibly respond in the negative. I do think, though, if by 'this country' we mean Catalonia, such a way of doing things would be viable, and soon everybody would be very satisfied as to the advantages it offers. On the other hand, if we mean Spain as a whole, the answer would be very different.

Just imagine. You would receive your registration form through the post, you would send it back with stamps purchased at the postal counter of your local tobacconist, shortly afterwards you would be notified of how much you owed in tax, and then, again by post, your certificate of payment would arrive after you had sent the due amount by postal order... Oh, dear! It would not work as simply as that. You would have to go all the way to the Head Post Office and stand in the queues there. You would waste almost as much time as you do when going through current procedures to obtain an identity card.

There is logic to all of this, though: in our complicated times, the simplest ways of organising things depend upon the most finely tuned organisations.

Paris, January 1929

I am in the National Library. My work finished, I picked up a volume – number IV – of Elisée Réclus's *Nouvelle Géographie Universelle*, with no particular aim in view. Sometimes, after having done a piece of absorbing, detailed work, I like to browse among books, carefree. Some marginal notes and pencil underlining on page 364 attracted my attention. Marked in this way was Réclus's opinion about the English character. Even though, according to the regulations, any reader caught underlining or writing notes in a book would lose his library card *ipso facto*, that distant reader of Réclus could not refrain from commenting on the geographer's words. Those few comments and that bit of underlining evoked a blazing reaction, prompted by the segment in question, a reaction ostensibly born of suffering and frustration. It was as though I could feel the pulsation of intense human pain, revived in that act of reading, and it hurt me to shut that pain up again on closing the book. I have copied out the passage from Réclus, together with the anonymous reader's underlining (shown here in italics) and comments (between parentheses). Both items are very interesting. The text reads as follows:

'Employée pour l'avantage personnel de l'individu dans la lutte de l'existence, l'énergie britannique est souvent accompagnée d'une VÉRITABLE FÉROCITÉ (oui!). L'Anglais sait écarter violemment ceux qui le *gênent pour s'ouvrir un chemin au milieu de la foule*. L'indépendance dont il est si fier n'est souvent autre chose qu'un *défaut absolu de sympathie pour autrui* (oui!). Il n'a qu'à suivre son inclination naturelle pour devenir (non: il est) dur, *froid, égoiste*. Même en face d'un inconnu, il a fréquemment (toujours) l'attitude d'un ennemi. Son histoire nationale raconte d'*épouvantables cruautés*, commises de sang-froid, d'une manière systématique et réfléchie, non comme en d'autres pays dans l'exaltation du fanatisme ou de la peure qui se venge. (I am not surprised.)

And now I am distracted by the thought that the reader and commentator of this passage from Réclus must have been a Frenchman (the hand-writing seems to be that of a man), more particularly a southern Frenchman: he had lived in England, he had struggled there, he had been defeated there. Defeated by both the people and the weather. I imagine that an almost unknown passage by Edmond Goncourt (*Les frères Zemganno*) would apply to him as one who:

'... prenait l'ennui d'Angleterre. Son tempérament latin avec ses ascendances en des contrées de soleil, commençait à avoir assez du brouillard de la Grande-Bretagne, de son ciel gris, de ses maisons enfumées, de cette atmosphere de charbon de terre pénétrant tout de sa crasse et faisant reconnaitre, à la première vue, des monnaies d'argent, qui, meme enfermées en des médaillers, ont séjourné quelques années dans ce pays de la triste et obscurante houille.'

And now – my imagination continues to run – having been reunited with his beloved France, enjoying a modest and undemanding leisure which allows him to wander into the library every now and then, in the peace and quiet of this room so well described by Rilke, absorbed in long-forgotten books, that anonymous defacer of the book relives his tragedy through the words of the geographer.

Are the geographer's words veracious, though? I think that they would not have been fair at the time they were written, and they would be even less so nowadays. The England of industrial cities creates a sense of strength that borders on hardness and imposes itself on you virtually all the time. A man who was not born and has not lived in that environment must be strong to put up unflinchingly with the effect of the climate, the food and, among the poorer classes, the housing. If to all of this must be added the struggle for survival, anyone who does not really belong will be easily cast aside: natural selection, despite all its progress and its benefit, is very harsh in such a country.

Paris, February 1929

Theatre audiences. – In spite of the common ground shared by all audiences (the common ground of belonging to the human race), every specific theatre-going public displays one or more features which distinguish it from its counterparts, according to geographical factors and also according to inherent social, intellectual or emotional characteristics. These features are not always readily discernible. Sometimes you can feel that there is a clear difference of mood, a certain nuance which differentiates a particular audience from other similar ones, but it will be very difficult to state what this nuance consists of: it is almost a matter of something in the atmosphere, subtle, perhaps indefinable. It is tempting, nevertheless, to seek conclusions which have some degree of substance and of solidity. The urge is as dangerous as it is tempting.

Giving way now to this temptation and announcing the danger beforehand as an excuse for possible errors, I would like to say a little on the subject mentioned above. There are few other situations involving an audience which lend themselves so readily to observation of two particular manifestations: laughter and applause. Serious emotion is more restrained and modest: the same person who easily bursts into loud laughter will force back any tear that might be welling up, and they will struggle hard to prevent any sudden lighting up of the auditorium from a surprising show of deep emotion which would betray weakness or cause embarrassment. On the other hand, it is most unusual to find anyone who feels this way about laughing openly: and being so contagious, much more than weeping, laughter will prevail loudly from the very moment that any group of people find reason to laugh. This is why one must distrust in principle excessively categorical opinions that would typify the theatre-going public of any particular country as being able to subdue and squeeze its laughter into a murmur. One of the biggest surprises I experienced in England, imbued as I was with the clichés concerning its inhabitants, was to discover that audiences there are among those most inclined to give free rein to their laughter. The typical English person will know how to laugh discreetly in their home, at their club, at social gatherings, but set him and a collection of compatriots in front of one of those hilarious comedy actors that they so delight in and that are never missing from any self-respecting variety company, and you will hear the great waves of laughter rolling out without any self-consciousness, sincere, healthy, endless. And, if you go into one of those music halls in popular neighbourhoods or in a typically working-class town, you will notice how laughter periodically rings out explosively from the men's mouths and in sharp long yells from the women's.

French audiences do not have, perhaps, such an easy or open way of laughing as English ones, but they are much freer with their applause. This applies not only to popular-theatre audiences, but also to those attending classical theatre performances. In France one needs to go to the so-called 'avant-garde' and 'art' theatres to find a noticeable reluctance, even sometimes an excessive resistance, to breaking into applause. Thus, for example, an English play has been running at L'Oeuvre[40] for Heaven knows how long (I think it must be nearing its hundredth performance), '*The Circle*' by Somerset Maugham. It is a delightful comedy, in which frivolity and depth, poetic and realistic touches, the pitch of both detail and total effect, are fused in perfect balance: one of the best plays of our times, I would dare say; one of those pieces designed to exasperate all thespians given to overacting. Almost every main role is well played by the members of the Lugnoe-Poe company; some parts could not be better fleshed out. The audience savours the work. Applause, though, is scarce throughout.

On the other hand, in mainstream theatres, the applause is often excessive when a play goes down well. The average Parisian feels obliged to punctuate each sentence that appeals to him by underlining it with vigorous clapping. Thus, the performance can be interrupted at every end and turn. Needless to say, this affects what is happening on stage, making it hard to enjoy the performance and destroying some of the effects cleverly contrived by the author. We can cite as typical the case of a current run of Corneille's *Horace*: the audience often shatters the effect of old Horace's climactic response by interrupting, with their applause, the magnificent string of alexandrines which culminate in that celebrated line:

Que vouliez-vous qu'il fît contre trois? – Qu'il mourût!

Nothing like this happens in England. It is unusual for a theatrical performance to be interrupted by clapping. I could count on the fingers of one hand the times that I have observed such a phenomenon there, so exceptional is it. Of course, we

40   Celebrated avant-garde theatre in central Paris opened in the late nineteenth century.

are not talking here about the music hall genre, which – we must not forget – is these days the most popular type of theatre in that country.

*

And what about the tradition of speech-making after the end of the play? Last year in our press there was a vigorous debate on the matter, already much discussed. One particular author, forced to speak in response to an enthusiastic audience's insistence, did so, but only to utter an anathema against this very custom. Everybody had their say in the papers, and everybody or almost everybody disagreed with him.

I followed the debate with great interest; more than anything because we were at that time residing in a country which often likes to demand a few curtain-call words to bring a performance to a conclusion. Since we are talking about a leading country – England – some of the negative comments directed by Catalan journalists against this quirk in our own theatre-going public, and some of the pessimistic conclusions they insisted on drawing, seemed quite out of place. It was obvious that few important conclusions could be based on the fact that people anywhere should favour rounding off a play with a couple of words delivered from the stage.

English audiences are in the habit of getting the actors to make speeches, a custom not yet widespread in Catalonia. The play is over, the audience, showing its satisfaction, goes on clapping and clapping; only a few people leave the auditorium. The cast that sometimes, depending on the company and the play – especially in revues and musicals – have come out one by one or in small groups to receive the audience's applause, are now gathered all together on stage. Faced with such insistent enthusiasm, after a moment's hesitation, the company director steps forward into the proscenium. 'I suppose,' he says, in so many words, 'that you all will agree to give a big round of applause to actor X, who has been the life and soul of the performance.' Actor X is, invariably, the one who, throughout the revue or the musical comedy, has kept the audience in a perpetual state of good-humoured satisfaction. Needless to say, the company director's invitation is accepted with diligent unanimity. Everybody applauds, those on stage as well as the audience. Actor X, to whom colleagues and audience pay such a big-hearted tribute, steps forward visibly moved. When silence is restored, he pronounces: 'Thank you, thank you very much.' The applause begins again, and everybody goes home to bed satisfied.

Events may, of course, unfold in other ways: we have, for example, the Shakespearian actor who, having played very hard to get, steps gracefully forward, and with a voice and a pose tinged with reticence or fatigue he explains ingratiatingly: 'Do please excuse me if I do not say much: I must keep up my strength for later tonight. We are performing *The Taming of the Shrew* and, as you will understand, I have a rather daunting task ahead of me.'

It may be, though, that events like these simply do not happen. For them to take place as just described, there has to have been a real empathy between the stage and the audience, and these paying clients have to be relatively unsophisticated. With such an audience, though, that kind of rapport is not difficult to achieve in England, given the kind of mix of the comic and the sentimental offered by popular writers and composers as well.

This means that when English theatregoers make the actors address them, their motivation is both naïve and completely sincere. They try hard not only to show a favourite actor how much they love him or her, but they also demand some words spoken by an individual to the audience en masse, without any mediation of the author or of stage convention. Maybe it is in this very sincerity that we could find a differential feature in comparison with Catalan audiences. When our theatregoers call the author on to the stage, or, once on stage, they oblige him to speak, everyone knows full well that what is involved is not always an outpouring of true enthusiasm. Curiosity, a certain maliciousness, sometimes just rowdy high spirits may contribute to the fictitious sensation of a fervour that is merely put on by those displaying it, and if the author were actually to hear what was being said about him and his smug delight, he would hurry to take shelter in the wings.

Then there could be this other difference: the English audience does not call out 'Speech!' nor anything similar: they just clap insistently, with a tenacity that contrasts with their reluctance to applaud on other occasions, even in cases of true success. The reason for this contrast is not always very evident. The kind of audience makes a difference, undoubtedly, but the dramatic genre is almost certainly a factor as well. In Catalonia, the same degree of enthusiasm can be produced by an operetta, a drama or a comedy. It seems to me that this is not so in England, or that at least the way enthusiasm or satisfaction are expressed changes according to genre. In my memory, a sharp contrast stands out between the ovations for the shabbiest revue in the most god-forsaken of theatres and the clapping for the finest of Shakespearian productions in the theatre of Stratford-on-Avon. Between these two bench-marks we would place all the other experiences we gleaned. And our conclusion would perhaps be that the usual type of lightweight English production does not call for, indeed even shuns, excessive applause. Undoubtedly, the humour that flows through such works invites either a smile or a sigh more than a burst of applause.

In conclusion, the moral tenor of the play has its own influence, perhaps not in the way the work is enjoyed, but certainly in the way it is responded to. The fact that English theatregoers, as much as any other audiences, revel in plays as risqué as *Potiphar's Wife* – the wife of a lord who tries to seduce their chauffeur – seems unquestionable to me. However, also just as clear is that, after having thoroughly enjoyed the play, their final judgement on it comes across as distinctly chilly, a reaction which nevertheless does not prevent the work from having a long run. Our Catalan public would not behave in this way, and far less – needless to say – would French audiences, which take in their stride the most indelicate situations and the most forthright language.

23 May 1929

The welcome King. – This name befits the present King of England, and it is to him that we are referring here. Now that he has been declared fully restored to health after five months of illness, it must be acknowledged that in our times there have been few manifestations of a people so solicitously concerned about the health and the life of their sovereign. Not many monarchs these days could pride themselves on meriting the affection of their subjects to the extent that this applies to King George V. From the conservatives to the socialists, from the grandest lord to the humblest villager, all the people of England have anxiously followed the vicissitudes of his distressing illness. Ramsay Macdonald, speaking in Paris to a working-class public in republican France, made explicit and heartfelt declarations of loyalty to the King, expressing sincere wishes for his return to full health. Lord Rothermere, in order to thank Heaven that his sovereign was cured, has recently sent the sum of 100,000 guineas to George V's secretary, to be deposited in the King Edward VII Fund for London hospitals, while thousands of lowly citizens have with touching innocence, for as long as the illness lasted, been sending all manner of contributions like suggestions for popular remedies, treasured family medicines, wholesome foodstuffs from the English countryside: eggs, poultry, butter, vegetables, all of which produce has filled pantry shelves in various London hospitals. Doubtless, if George V had been able to eat of this fare, he would have done so without second thoughts or scruples. The scenario is reminiscent of that passage in his Chronicle where Ramon Muntaner voices his eulogy of the Catalan Kings:[41] 'Furthermore, if any person of rank, knight, prelate, burgher, man of standing, country dweller or other individual sends fruit, wine or other things to them, there is no doubt they will eat these things…'

41   Ramon Muntaner (1265-1336): one of the four great chroniclers of the period when the Catalans exercised extensive dominion throughout the Mediterranean. Strong patriotism resonates throughout the writing and Muntaner's style is celebrated for its distinctly literary ambition.

The English press has faithfully reflected the feelings of the people: medical bulletins published under banner headlines, specialised comments on the bulletins, detailed accounts of the silent displays of support for the monarch and of interest in his state of health, photographs of the crowds waiting to read the announcements displayed on the railings of Buckingham Palace; then – with the King having entered a phase of encouraging improvement, when his doctors announced as more or less imminent his transfer to Aldwick, close to Bognor in Sussex – detailed optimistic accounts of the excellent facilities at Craigwell House, the convalescent home selected for him; comments on the climatologic advantages of the location, one of the sunniest places in England, and comments too on the wonderful effects of sunlight and sea air on repairing the patient's organism and on rebuilding his strength: all of this conveyed with the special affection with which the English talk about the sun – a guest much admired because so often absent – and when they talk about the seaside, a presence much admired because of being so familiar.

In the hours of greatest anxiety, when the death of George V seemed inevitable, the words of *God save the King* must have been responded to with extreme unction throughout the land, sung as this anthem is at the end of every public entertainment. I thought initially that this custom was quite ridiculous, almost grotesque when experienced in a tatty back-street theatre at the end of a particularly trivial, vulgar revue: the orchestra which had assailed our ear-drums with its infernal noises solemnly struck up the opening bars of the national anthem, with the whole audience standing, heads uncovered, meditative to a degree. The contrast is all the more disconcerting because this does not actually bring the show to its conclusion. No sooner have the closing notes faded than the orchestra charges at full pelt through the craziest and most raucous musical item from the show which has just ended. Even so, the moving devotion shown by the English people towards their monarch, as evinced in the circumstance of his illness, demonstrates the extent to which this ritual, apparently a mere routine, at odds with the setting and slightly grotesque, does have a real content of strong and heartfelt emotion.

King George himself, for his part, has effectively played to these feelings with the message he addressed to the whole British Empire:

'Thinking about my illness,' he said, 'my heart is filled with a gratitude the origin of which is much deeper than the feeling of relief at being restored to health. Thanks to medical science and to the untiring efforts of my doctors and nurses, the danger I was in is now behind me. Help came also from another source. As the months went by, I became increasingly aware of the affection surrounding the Queen and myself. In my thoughts now I can see my friends who were waiting in large numbers outside my room in the hospital, and the even larger number of those who in every part of the British Empire were thinking of me in their prayers.'

'It has been one of the most vivid experiences of my whole life. It was for me an indescribable encouragement to feel that my most constant vow, the most serious one of all, to win the confidence and the love of my people, had been realised.'

Beyond this the royal message contains mention of the warm sympathy displayed towards him by numerous unknown friends in countries outside the Empire. And he concludes by expressing confidence that the day is not far away when he, along with his people, will be able to thank God Almighty for his return to health.

What we are witnessing, then – at a time when the institution of monarchy itself is in deep crisis, shortly after the Great War has swept away a good number of thrones, sceptres and crowns – is a priceless popular consecration of the crown worn by the Plantagenets, the Stuarts and the house of Hanover. It must be remembered that this crown had slipped more than once on the heads of those who wore it, and that it had fallen more than once, on one occasion when the head itself which wore it was removed. The vicious joke made by a wily old English ambassador comes naturally to mind:

'*Vous sacrez les rois en Angleterre?*'

'*Oui, Sire: et nous les massacrons aussi*'[42]

Perhaps this was an essential condition in order to arrive at the present-day fellow feeling that exists between English people and their sovereigns.

42   I have been unable to discover the origin of this boutade.